P9-CCT-838

SHARPENING
THE
WARRIOR'S EDGE

Bruce K. Siddle

© Bruce K. Siddle, 1995
Distributed by PPCT Research Publications
PPCT Management Systems, Inc.
7645 Magna Drive
2nd Floor
Belleville, IL 62223
ph# 618-234-PPCT (7728)

ISBN#0-9649205-0-6

First Printing: October 1995
Second Printing: September 1996
Third Printing: March 1998
Fourth Printing: January 2000
Fifth Printing: January 2001
Sixth Printing: May 2003
Seventh Printing: February 2005
Eighth Printing: September 2005
Ninth Printing: August 2006
Tenth Printing: March 2008

Dedication

To my wife Sandy and my sons, Jonathan and Kevin, I dedicate this book with all my love. Without their support, I would not be where I am today. Nor, would I want to be where I am today without them.

In loving memory of
Catherine Siddle
who left this earth on March 24, 1995.

We look forward to seeing you again Grandma,
in Eternity.

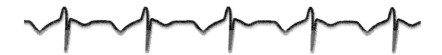

Table of Contents

Sharpening the Warrior's Edge

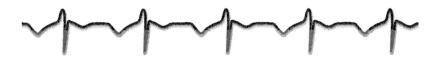

Acknowledgments

S *harpening the Warrior's Edge* is a product of eight year's research. Throughout this time, a number of individuals have provided a wide range of support which contributed to the content of this text.

To Professors Harold Johnson, Jack Seitzinger, Vance McLaughlin and Darrell Ross, thank you for teaching me the importance of research, validation and challenging the status quo.

More than any outside source, Ed Lovette became a principal contributor to the development of this text. His motivation kept me focused during the difficult periods of research and writing. But, most importantly, his dedication to enhancing survival is "the" model of professionalism.

I would especially like to thank Dave Smith, who helped me conceptualize this text, and who will be recorded as one of the most important survival instructors of this generation.

Desmond Morrison became very pivotal to the subsequent research on condition response training principles. As my mentor and "surrogate stepfather" he has patiently kept me focused on the need for simplicity and environmental inoculation.

Paul Whitesell, Ph.D. helped me recognize the importance of studying the relationship between anxiety/survival stress and the heart rate. But more importantly, he inspired me to study the warrior mindset by his example.

Dr. Hal Breedlove became very important to the development of chapters four and six. I consider his research on stress and visual systems to be the cutting edge of survival and combat performance. It is very rare to find a practicing professional, outside of this community, who contributes without hesitation.

The tactical firearms research would not have been complete without the assistance of Col. Rex Applegate, Aubrey Futrell, Steel Parsons, Russell Tanji and Bill Burroughs.

I will never be able to fully acknowledge the assistance of PPCT Staff Instructors Mike Dunn, Mike Kerby, Tom Hontz, Steel Parsons and Harland Westmoreland. These friends have patiently provided content editorial support in their respective specialties.

As the primary content editor, Mark Dunston became a principal figure in the last year of writing. His contributions and friendship have become very important to me and my family.

Nancy Glaeser, a teacher and new mother, found time to grammatically edit this text.

Acknowledgments

Utilizing their incredible talents, the staff of Heeley Creative, Inc. took the theme of the text and turned it into the cover.

The single most important contributor to this project and my life, is my wife Sandy. Through twenty years of marriage, she has become a crucial component in motivating and supporting me in my efforts to advance the professionalism of this field. Any legacy which I leave behind is due to our partnership.

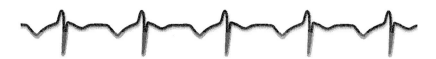

Introduction

"Untutored courage is useless in the face of educated bullets."

General George S. Patton

E nhancing human performance has gained consider-
able attention in the last two decades.
Once the exclusive domain of athletics, the search
for the performance edge is now considered to be the
pinnacle of individual success.

Ironically, the search for the performance edge is not
a new concept. The warrior class has recognized the
existence of a higher plane of combat performance for
thousands of years. It is a level of performance where
physical skills are precisely executed with little effort.
Cognitive processing becomes so efficient that the perception of time distorts and the warrior experiences virtually no
fear or anxiety.

There is no doubt among warriors that peak combat
performance zones do exist. However, understanding the

scientific physiology of this phenomenon has remained elusive and misunderstood.

In 1984, the Army Research Institute asked the National Academy of Sciences to explore a variety of techniques which were proposed to enhance human performance. A committee was established in 1985 of distinguished scientists from a variety of psychological sciences and the field of cognitive neuroscience. The goal of this committee was to scientifically examine methods of learning which could prepare a soldier for combat or for complex technical operations.

The committee examined a wide range of so called accelerated learning and performance techniques, referred to as "new age" learning techniques. The results are well documented in *Enhancing Human Performance: Issues, Theories and Techniques* (1988) and *In the Mind's Eye* (1991). Although the committee's research into new age learning techniques is exhaustive and comprehensive, they failed to identify procedures which could be immediately and simply implemented for the average soldier/officer.

Another attempt to explore advanced training methods is *"The Warrior's Edge"*, (Alexander, Groller and Morris, 1990). This excellent text reviewed a variety of enhanced performance principles. Not only did the authors examine new age learning techniques, but they also examined a series of practical techniques such as breathing, martial arts training and the warrior mindset.

Yet, a true profile on the physiology of survival stress and combat performance has not surfaced. Instructors, soldiers and officers do not have a reference that clearly identifies the affects of survival stress on performance and why skills deteriorate. More importantly, the art of training warriors has not been elevated to a science, with standard design methodologies based upon scientific research.

Sharpening the Warrior's Edge will hopefully be viewed as the next evolution to establishing the science of training warriors. This text is a culmination of eight years research into educational psychology, neurobiology, motor learning sciences and thousands of hours in the classroom training today's warriors (criminal justice officers and members of the special operations and special warfare community). My goal is to unwrap some of the mysteries surrounding combat and survival performance, with the ultimate goal of enhancing the survival of today's warriors.

Sharpening the Warrior's Edge will focus on the relationship between survival stress, escalating heart rates and combat performance. This relationship creates a combat paradox, a state where a "perceived" high-threat stimulus automatically engages the sympathetic nervous system. The activation of this system increases the heart rate, which in turn has a crucial affect on motor performance, visual processing and cognitive reaction time. For example, at 115 beats per minute (BPM), fine motor skills (precision and accuracy skills) deteriorate. When the heart rate exceeds 145 BPM, complex motor skills deteriorate and the visual system begins to narrow. But when the heart rate exceeds 175 BPM, a warrior can expect to experience auditory exclusion and the loss of peripheral vision and depth perception. This initiates a catastrophic failure of the cognitive processing capabilities, leading to fatal increases in reaction time or hypervigilance (freezing in place or irrational acts).

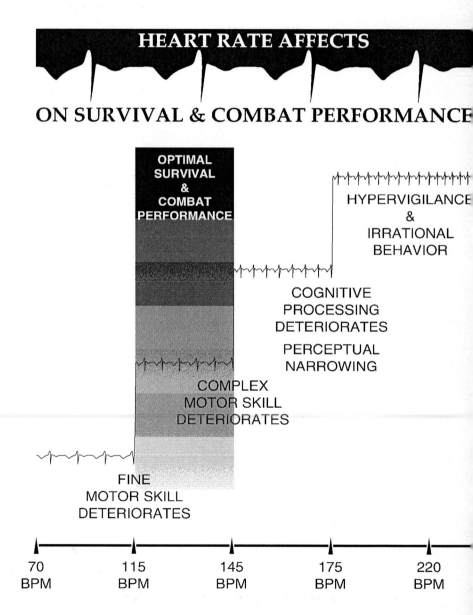

This research provides a rational explanation for the discrepancies often observed between the classroom and the field, and explains why some skills are not compatible to survival stress environments. Therefore, the focal point of *Sharpening the Warrior's Edge* is controlling the heart rate.

The first two chapters examine a specific training psychology, which proposes that all training should be directed at developing skill confidence. These chapters suggest that a mindset free of anxiety or fear will indirectly control escalating heart rates and increase combat effectiveness. Chapter two becomes more specific, by examining principles of neural learning to enhance survival reaction time.

Chapters three and four explore how stress affects motor skills and reaction time. These chapters provide a clear foundation of research needed to design and validate survival and combat systems.

Chapter five identifies the mechanisms of survival stress are identified and explores how anxiety or fear initiates the sympathetic nervous system, which begins a catastrophic spiral in motor and cognitive functions. The chapter will also address a series of design and practical survival stress management techniques.

Attempting to put the research into perspective, chapter six describes the process of selecting and implementing the survival learning research. I found this chapter difficult to write, for the readers of this text will range from military personnel, criminal justice officers, special operations units and a number of other high risk groups. Subsequently, I needed a common ground which each of the warrior specialties would find applicable to their environment. I selected the development of a tactical firearms system for building entries. This is a common activity for all of the above.

The final chapter explores the warrior's mindset. This chapter has special meaning to me personally. Chapter seven examines a series of mindsets that not only maintain low heart rates, but also prepare warriors for combat.

I tried to make this text user friendly so that the reader can skip to the chapters considered most relevant. Each chapter will have overlapping themes, focusing on creating confidence, selecting simple/gross motor skills and the role of the heart rate on performance. I also used the term "student" generically, instead of soldier, officer or operator.

Sharpening the Warrior's Edge is written in honor of the warrior class, who protect their communities and country with their lives.

Bruce K. Siddle

Introduction References

Alexander, J., Groller, R., and Morris, J. (1990)
    The Warrior's Edge, Morrow Publishing
National Research Council, (1988) *Enhancing Human
    Performance*: National Academy Press
National Research Council, (1991) *In the Mind's Eye*:
    National Academy Press

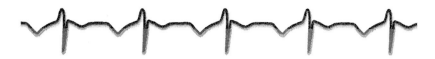

1

The Psychology of Survival Training

"A great teacher speaks the language of emotions — by inspiring and motivating. . ."

Dan Millman, 1979

Since the beginning of strategic warfare, a special group of individuals has been tasked with training warriors to survive in combat. This profession over ten thousand years old has influenced the rise and fall of nations throughout history. It is the only recognized profession that trains students to protect lives by taking another life at the same time. It is also one of the few professions in which the instructor's competence may be the difference between the life and death of the student or the general public.

Throughout the centuries, survival training has changed very little. Survival instructors have struggled with the lack of resources and the necessary time to adequately train their students. Even with today's advanced weapon systems and technology, instructors must compensate for human limitations.

Instructors who teach survival skills (i.e. defensive tactics, close-quarter combat, tactical firearms, or survival strategies) are still faced with teaching students a physical skill. The author proposes the level of student proficiency is directly proportionate to the instructor's training psychology and system design. Subsequently, instructors have a moral and legal obligation to constantly research methods to enhance training and, ultimately, to assure the survival of their students.

Unlike other motor skill training, survival skills will be performed in the stress of combat. As such, motor skill training inherits a fair degree of learning and performance limitations. Although the learning roadblocks are multiple, there are three constant variables which directly affect survival and combat training. First, is the development of a system of skills which are appropriate for the arena of performance. For example, skills need to be designed to control specific threat stimuli. Second, the instructional delivery system must ensure that the students can learn and develop confidence in the skill quickly. The final variable recognizes that the influence of motivational principles has a direct effect on the student's training intensity and subsequent skill development.

The three elements of system design selection presentation skills, and motivation principles, become the basis of a training psychology. Exceptional instructors are conscious of their unique educational role. These instructors understand the limitations often associated with training. They make the most of the training time and resources allocated. They understand the limitations of the average student's abilities. Finally, they understand the connection between training motivation, developing technique confidence, and the successful use of a "learned" skill in the stress of combat.

The instructor's ultimate goal is to develop the student's technique fluidity under the stress of combat. Therefore, it becomes critical to study the research findings and literature that already exist in the motor learning sciences.

Even though the study of motor skill behavior is over a century old, the study of survival motor skills has been slow to develop. Except for a select few individuals throughout the last forty years, most motor skill research has been in the fields of industrial and sports psychology. The study of motor skills in any field is dedicated to advancing the individual's overall performance. Survival skills training has only one specific goal—enhancing survival skills.

There have been many different definitions of a "skill." Psychologist E. R. Guthrie (1952) stated that "a skill consists of the ability to bring about some end result with maximum certainty and minimum outlay of energy, or of time and energy." Although it is reasonable to assume that Guthrie did not have survival skills in mind when this definition was written, the definition nevertheless identifies the two very important elements of survival training: *maximum certainty and minimal outlay of energy.* Schmidt (1991) observes of Guthrie's definition, "This minimum-energy notion applies to organizing the action not only so the physiological energy costs are lower, but also the psychological or mental energy required is reduced. Many skills have been learned so well that the performers hardly have to pay attention to them, freeing their cognitive processes for other features of the activity." Schmidt later identifies three skill-performance goals based upon the findings of Guthrie's work. They are as follows:

- Maximizing the achievement certainty.
- Minimizing the physical and mental energy costs of the performance.
- Minimizing the time used.

The subsequent definition of a survival motor skill would be any defensive or preemptive motor skill designed to protect human life. To ensure performance efficiency, the skill should be designed to include the following:

- A maximum certainty of success to maintain high survivability.
- A minimal outlay of physical or mental energy, so the skill would be applicable in any environment.
- Minimal reaction and response time or simplicity in technique application.

Are the instructor's physical skills important? Certainly, but only to a point. Consider the training an Olympic athlete receives from his coach. Olympic coaches rarely have the abilities of their students. But through the use of videos, training aids, and demonstration components of a skill in slow motion, they can motivate and train athletes to exceptional levels of performance. Therefore, exceptional instructors are distinguished not by their physical abilities, but by their ability to motivate and train students to perform a specific skill in a specific environment.

Exceptional instructors have the ability to create a learning cycle that is constantly feeding upon itself. *In the center of this cycle is the goal of creating and increasing the student's confidence in a specific set of skills.* Confidence minimizes the physiological affects of stress and places the student in a physical parameter for optimum combat performance. In fact, the author has hypothesized that if students do not have a subconscious confidence factor for a survival skill, the students will never use the skill in the stress of combat.

What contributes to the development of skill confidence? This text will suggest that confidence is a result of the instructor's training methodology. The training methodology is based upon four steps designed to create skill confidence by motivating the students to learn and practice: creating a need to learn the skill; convincing the students they can learn the skill quickly; creating an environment where the students observe the skill working; and providing the students with firsthand experience which ingrains a high potential of success. Thus, training psychology becomes the critical element of the learning cycle of survival training.

Motivational Factors of Learning

The previous section proposed a hypothesis stipulating that learned survival responses are a product of a specific training methodology. The basis of this methodology is developing the student's confidence in a skill at a subconscious level. However, motivating the students to "want to learn" can often be more difficult than learning the skill itself. Therefore, understanding how to motivate students to learn and practice a skill becomes an intrinsic component of training.

Motivating students to practice is as important as developing technique confidence. Schmidt (1991) observed, "A student who is not motivated at all will not practice, and little or no learning will result. A motivated student devotes greater effort to the task, with more serious practice and longer practice periods, leading to more effective learning."

The author's study of exceptional instructors has found that their motivation skills are often superior to their physical teaching skills. They are not only entertaining and enjoyable to listen to, but they demonstrate a knowledge of a topic which students find fascinating, interesting, and relevant to a specific need. In essence, exceptional instructors are so because of their motivational abilities.

The interaction between developing the student's confidence and motivating students to learn creates the basis of a training psychology. This psychology is a constantly evolving learning cycle: *Motivation to learn motivates the student to practice a skill. A commitment to practice leads to an increased awareness and a mental state to achieve high skill levels. High skill levels lead to technique confidence.* The author (Siddle, 1991) believes this learning cycle is based upon four motivational factors which act as the basis of motivating students to learn survival and combat skills. They are as follows:

Create a need for the skill: Creating a need to learn a survival skill is the first essential element of motivation. When an instructor creates a need to learn, the students understand that there is an immediate or future need for the skill. This acceptance of the need will in turn create an open mindset and willingness. Furthermore, if the instructor presents a skill which makes sense, the students will be "committed" to attempt to learn or practice the skill. In turn, practice creates technique competence and fluidity, which leads to technique confidence.

Creating a need for a skill in survival training can be

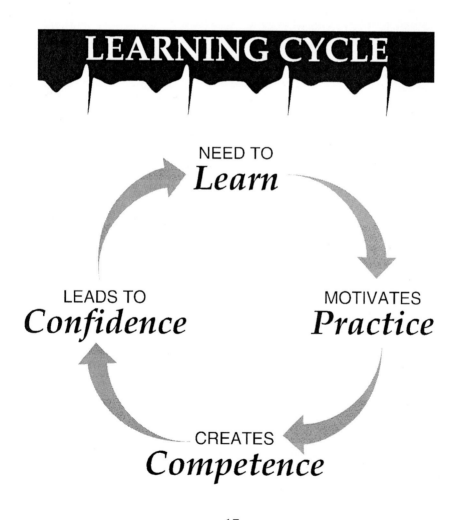

LEARNING CYCLE

NEED TO
Learn

MOTIVATES
Practice

CREATES
Competence

LEADS TO
Confidence

accomplished by showing the students reports or studies of how the skills will be used to control specific threat behavior. This motivator can be especially strong when the "need" relates to the survival of the student. However, instructors must make sure the "need" makes sense. Too many times instructors attempt to teach a survival skill that the average student cannot visualize ever needing in the field. Subsequently, the students must be able to visualize the skill's real-life applications.

Students must believe they can learn the skills quickly: Most of us have experienced training in which we arrive motivated to learn but become frustrated because skill competence cannot be achieved quickly. This can occur even if the students understand that the skill is essential to survival.

When the students begin to believe that a skill is not achievable, the most common reason is that the instructor's method of presentation is unclear. Instructors of survival skills often forget that students learn a skill through a principle called *modeling.* In essence, modeling begins when the instructor demonstrates the skill. The instructor's presentation is processed in the brain in the form of a picture. The students consciously and subconsciously visualize the demonstration in their mind's eye. Based upon this picture, a neural motor program begins to form. However, the student's learning speed and skill level will be directly proportional to the instructor's ability to create clear pictures, which the students replicate.

To maintain high training motivation levels, the instructor must convince the students they can learn a skill quickly. Every aspect of an instructor's articulation and physical skill demonstration should be directed toward minimizing student frustration. Instruction methods to enhance the student's ability to learn quickly are as follows:

• *The instructor should never demonstrate a technique or a skill beyond 50% in speed or power.* This demonstration principle is designed for students who are learning a skill for the first time. Instructors often forget that new students do not have the base knowledge enabling them to consciously "see" the fine points of a skill. By demonstrating a skill at half speed, the student's eye will have a better opportunity to track the components of a skill. In essence, the mind's eye will have a better chance of capturing a complete picture for motor program replication.

• *When a skill is introduced, the instructor should demonstrate and teach each skill in three separate components: the beginning, the middle, and the end.* It is not uncommon to have a student become frustrated because he cannot coordinate the many components of a skill. This can be avoided by splitting the technique into three separate components and teaching each component as an individual skill. This procedure allows the student to concentrate on one component at a time, without the distractions of the second and third components. Instructors who adopt this procedure will find that student frustration is kept to a minimum and training motivation remains high.

• *All verbal feedback should be directed at clarifying the mental pictures.* When instructors give the students feedback, they should remember that the purpose of feedback is to correct and refine the neural motor program. Subsequently, the instructor's feedback should be very specific and not overwhelming in the number of corrections.

Correction feedback should be focused on one mistake at a time. This element is very important in avoiding student confusion and frustration. It is not uncommon to see an instructor correct a student by pointing out several mistakes in the technique execution. Remember that feedback (verbal or demonstrative) creates a mental picture in the mind's eye of the student. This picture will be compared to the existing picture or neural motor program. Once the student comprehends the correction, he will change the mental picture, which automatically begins the changes with the neural motor program. However, if the instructor's feedback consists of multiple corrections, the mental picture will lack clarity, slowing down the learning process and increasing student frustration. Therefore, correction feedback should be focused on one component at a time. This allows the student to mentally process and correct that flaw before moving on to the next correction in the technique. Following this feedback procedure will not only diffuse student frustration, but also increase technique proficiency and confidence.

The students must have a positive training experience quickly: "The skill works fine in the static training environment, but will the skill work in the stress of combat?" This is a common critique applied to survival skills. This critique implies that the instructor's presentation was confusing or unclear. If this attitude is allowed to continue, the instructor will begin to see the student's level of motivation deteriorate.

Exceptional instructors recognize the relationship between motivation, technique, confidence and the level of achievement. Achievement implies a level of skill that can be measured in technique fluidity, and the amount of confidence the students have utilizing the skill in combat. Unfortunately, perceptions of technique complexity or applicability may interfere with developing a sense of achievement.

How can trainers combat this perception? The answer appears to be linked to the design of the system and the method of student practice. If the system design is based upon easy to learn techniques, then confidence and skill levels are quickly established. In addition, if the form of practice reinforces the effectiveness of the technique, then the student's subconscious confidence also increases. The subsequent goal is to create a training environment in which the students will have a positive training experience quickly. Considerations to meet this goal are as follows:

• *The students must learn the basic components of the skill within three minutes or twenty-five practice repetitions.* This chapter has continuously stressed the importance of the students learning a skill quickly. This strategy can, in part, be established through presentation skills which help the students mentally process the skill for replication. Unfortunately, the design of some survival skills can inherently be so complex that the skill is unsuitable to be learned quickly.

The study of motor behavior classifies motor skills into three basic forms. They are gross, fine, and complex motor skills. A gross motor skill is most commonly defined as a strength event which uses the major muscle masses, such as the arms and legs. Normally, a gross motor skill is a pushing or pulling event and is enhanced when adrenal action is involved. The second classification is fine motor skills. Fine motor skills involve hand-eye coordination and often some form of digital action. Unlike gross motor skills, adrenaline and stress will interfere with the fluidity and precision of fine motor skills. The final form is complex motor skills. Complex motor skills are a series of motor skills combined. Research (discussed in later chapters) has identified that complex motor skills have a parameter of optimal performance, that has been charted at a working heart rate between 115-145 beats per minute.

Research and common sense indicate that the average student will learn a gross motor skill at a much quicker rate than fine or complex motor skills. Research also indicates that gross motor skills are performed at optimal levels under high-stress conditions. In contrast, fine and complex motor skills deteriorate under high-stress conditions.

From the standpoint of survival skills training, gross motor skills are almost always easier to learn. The average gross motor skill can be learned in three minutes or less, or within twenty-five practice repetitions. If this design concept can be followed, then it stands to reason that students will gain confidence and have a positive training experience at a quicker rate.

• *The students must see the technique work.* An essential element of gaining confidence is having a positive experience quickly during the training process. Although this is common sense, a visual demonstration of a technique's effectiveness is very important in developing subconscious confidence.

• *The students must experience the technique personally, when possible.* Not all survival skills are conducive to this teaching principle. But when applicable, an instructor should have his students experience the correct and incorrect ramifications of a technique or skill. By giving the students firsthand knowledge of the correct application, the students know the intricacies of how the technique should be applied in the field. In contrast, when the students have firsthand knowledge of an incorrect technique, they will have a base understanding that will allow them to rationalize a technique's failure.

Students must have a positive field experience: The final factor needed to develop technique confidence is for the students to have a positive experience in a dynamic or field application. Attempts at dynamic training have improved considerably over the last decade with the advent of simulators, firearms training projectiles, and safety equipment used for empty-hand control practice. However, the effectiveness of dynamic training often deteriorates when the scenarios are not realistic or not based upon actual field applications. When this occurs, the student's motivation to practice the skill falls and eventually leads to a loss of confidence.

Chapter One Summary

Training students in survival skills is a very unique profession. This field is affected by variables which other sciences and educational fields seldom face. This constant reality has led some instructors to believe that we could never consider this field a science. The author acknowledges these facts but believes the key to being a professional is accepting the variables and designing the training systems based upon research.

This chapter has attempted to identify a training psychology which centers on enhancing survival performance through a systematic learning cycle. The ultimate goal of this training psychology is to develop the student's confidence at a subconscious level. The author contends that the relationship between motivation, practice intensity, skill competence, and skill confidence are inseparable and linked to one another. However, maintaining the student's motivation will be dependent upon the system design and the instructor's ability to present skills which can be learned quickly.

Chapter One References

Guthrie, E.R.(1952) *The Psychology of Learning*: Harper & Row.
Pargman, Dan. (1986). *Stress and Motor Performance: Understanding and Coping.*
Millman, Dan. (1979). *The Warrior Athlete.*
Rose, Colin. (1987) *Accelerated Learning*: Dell Publishing.
Schmidt, Richard A. (1991). *Motor Learning and Performance*, Human Kinetics.
Siddle, Bruce. (1991). *Survival Learning Theory Instructional Outline*, PPCT Management Systems, Inc.

2
The Neural Basis of Survival Motor Programs

"Learning can best be defined as a behavioral change that meets two criteria: it results from an experience and it endures over time."

Schneider, A. and Tarshis, B., 1986

No matter how simple a survival skill appears to be on the surface, the reality is that all intentional physical skills are highly complex neurophysiological functions of the human body. Exactly how the mind and body coordinate a motor skill of any type is still not completely understood by scientists. This becomes even more complicated when we attempt to understand a more specific field, such as the behavior and the training of people for the stress of combat. Nevertheless, the advancement into the neural mechanisms of learning has begun to provide insights which can be easily transferred to survival and combat training.

The study of learning is a highly complex field. Educators of any field face a variety of social, physical, and mental factors, which will have an impact on the student's ability and speed of learning new information. Survival instructors must handle all of these issues, plus the moral and psychological ramifications of surviving a deadly-force encounter. Students do not have the element of time to research an answer to the task at hand. Thus, methods of instruction must be found which will reduce the student's reaction time without the research time element.

The author acknowledges that the learning ability of students will be affected by a multitude of variables. Many of these variables will have been a result of socioeconomic environments and personal values which have been in-grained throughout their lifetime. These variables are of a nature which cannot be addressed by the average survival instructor. However, there are other avenues of learning which will have a positive affect on the processing speed and physical reaction time to a threat.

The Neurological Basis of Memory and Motor Programs

A number of theories over the last three decades speculate as to the potential of the human brain. In the past, scientists often stated that humans utilize about 10% of their brain's potential. But now as brain research is progressing, new theories estimate that man uses less than 4% of his potential brain power. That leaves 96% of the brain's learning resources untapped. Imagine human potential if we could increase the learning capabilities of the brain by just 2%.

The complexity of the brain's ability to process and store new information alone is almost beyond comprehension for the average individual. But scientists continue to research the brain for answers that pertain not only to physiological and psychological answers, but also for answers to advance the speed and capabilities of different technologies. For example, consider the field of artificial intelligence. Research in artificial intelligence began in the early 1950s as computer science moved out of its infancy stage. By the mid-1950s, scientists began to explore the possibilities of artificial intelligence to increase the efficiency and service capabilities of computers - specifically in robotics. Even though scientists were able to develop robots having arms and hands with gripping abilities, they soon discovered developing spatial and perceptual skills were another matter.

Today, robotics researchers are working closely with brain researchers. One of the top scientists in this field is Hans Moravec, Director of Mobile Robot Laboratory at Carnegie-Mellon. His research in robot intelligence has led him to some incredible findings of the visual processing abilities of the brain and motor coordinating functions. Moravec (1992) states, "Our perceptual motor circuitry, you know, is really very efficient. . . It's highly optimized, it's very large, and by my calculation, it does the equivalent effective computing of about 10 trillion computations per second. . . I've done a calculation about what it would take to duplicate human vision, mostly based upon the amount of nerve tissue involved and the efficiency that's displayed by the retina. The number I get is something like a trillion computations per second. . . So for a machine to perform a motor test, like playing tennis, you probably need a computer with no less than about, well, for a whole nervous system, 10 trillion computations per second. So you probably won't have a really good robot tennis player until you get that many computations per second to process all the sensory data and other things."

Scientists have found that the human nervous system begins to develop within twenty days of conception, and at five weeks the human brain begins development. At eight weeks neuroblasts (embryonic cells which eventually turn into neurons) are developing at a rate of several thousand per minute. Twelve weeks after conception, the brain is producing new neurons at a rate of 2,000 per second; by the time the infant is eighteen weeks before birth, the human embryo has developed the entire nervous system of 12 to 15 billion neurons. By adulthood the brain will have 12 to 15 billion nerve cells.

Approximately ten weeks before birth, each neuron begins to send out a series of thin fibers, attempting to make connections with other neurons. These connections become critical to the development of the brain's power, since the number of connections will determine the level of mental ability. "Since each neuron can, itself, make thousands of connections, the potential number of interconnections in the brain runs into the trillions. The key point to remember is that only some of these connections are made automatically. Most are made by using the brain. The more your brain is stimulated, the richer the connections and the higher the practical mental ability" (Rose, 1987).

Researchers now believe the functions of learning and memory are directly related to the connections between the neurons of the brain. "According to the dominant view of neuroscience that has developed over the last few decades, the brain is indeed a kind of computer, but only in a general sense. In fact, it sometimes seems more revealing to think of a single neuron as a little computer and the brain as a network of tens of billions of these information processing cells. Each neuron receives electrical impulses through a treelike structure called a dendrite, whose thousands of tiny branches funnel signals into the body of the cell. In computer jargon, the dendrite is the neuron's input device. While some of the arriving signals stimulate the neuron, others inhibit it. If the pluses exceed the minuses, the neuron fires, sending its own pulse down the stalk called an axon. The axon is the output channel. It feeds through junctions called synapses into the dendrites of other cells. The resulting circuitry is complex beyond imagination. A single neuron can receive signals from thousands of neurons; its axon can branch repeatedly, sending signals to thousands more" (Johnson, 1991).

The foundation of memory seems to be based upon the repeated firing between the connectors or dendrites. It appears that when the brain is exposed to a new stimulus or experience, a complex pattern of neurons is somehow activated, which is known as a program. When a new learning experience or program occurs, the signal has a difficult time jumping the synaptic gap. But as the new program is reintroduced by repetition or a strong association, the ability of the signal to cross the synaptic gap becomes easier.

Keeping in mind that memory is based upon recognition or recall, it appears that the basis of memory is encompassed by two issues. The first pertains to a substance called myelin. Myelin is a fatty protein which the brain releases to coat the connection between two dendrites as new information is learned. "This happens the first time a connection is made, and thereafter, anytime there is a proper stimulus from the environment to activate that connection again. . . At the time of the connection, it takes a lot of energy to 'get' it. After that it gets easier and easier as the myelin forms a thicker coat. Eventually, with enough repetition, the connection becomes sufficiently 'myelinated' and able to operate without effort while other connections are made" (Deporter, B. and Hernacki, M., 1992). The second basis of memory is the number of associations that stimulate the program. Obviously, the more associations that encompass several perceptual senses (sight, sound, smell, taste, and touch), the more the strength of the program will be enhanced.

The Neural Basis of Survival Response Programs

The foundation of survival training is based upon two principles. The first is the development of a survival program (skill) which controls a specific level of threat that the student can learn quickly. The speed at which a new survival program is learned will be based upon a number of variables, such as the complexity of the skill, how the skill was presented to the student, and whether the skill is truly applicable for the dynamic applications (these issues will be examined in future chapters.) However, we do know that all neural programs are strengthened the more a program is repeated due the increased myelination of the axons. As the myelination increases, so does the fluidity and speed of the technique.

Survival training, therefore, is the process of developing and refining a neural motor program, or for the purpose of survival and combat training, a *survival motor program.*

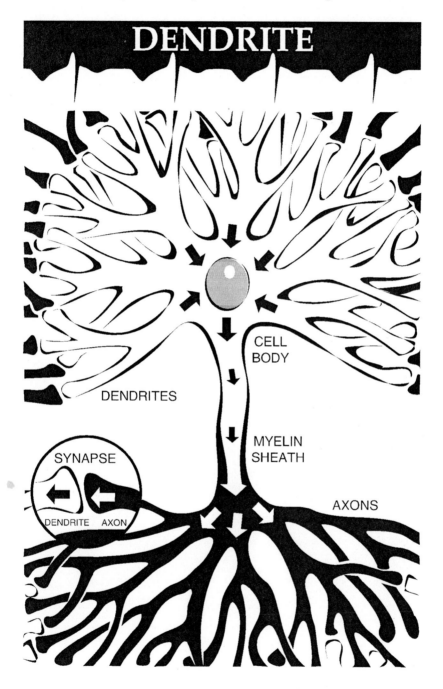

This instructional principle proposes that teaching any motor skill is a process of developing a mental picture in the mind's eye of the student. This picture leads to the development of a survival motor program which is downloaded to the central nervous system. Subsequently, every aspect of survival skills instruction should be directed at developing the survival motor program quickly. Issues to consider would include the following:

•   *Technique Presentation:* The average student learns a skill by observing the instructor's demonstration of the technique. The neural programming begins as the student watches the instructor demonstrate the skill, thus creating a picture of the skill in the mind's eye (short term sensory store). As the student mentally processes the picture in his mind's eye, the neural program begins to seek out appropriate connections with other nerve cells. The author refers to this process as *soft wiring.* Slowly, the neural program continues to be refined until the student attempts a physical application of the technique.

In many ways, there will be a direct relationship to the student's skill level and the instructor's demonstration skills. An instructor's demonstration creates a mental picture from which the student's survival program originates. Therefore, demonstration skills should be carefully articulated and presented so the mind's eye can develop a clear picture to replicate. (This concept will be explored further in following chapters.)

•   *Physical Skill Practice*: Chapter one explored the training principle which advocates structuring all physical practice sessions, so the student will gain technique confidence quickly. Developing confidence will be largely dependent upon the student seeing an increase in skill level or actually experiencing a successful technique application. In either case, confidence and technique success will be a product of technique fluidity. Technique fluidity is a result of the neural program refinement, or *hard wiring*. Hard wiring is the neural networking which occurs when the survival motor program moves from the visualization phase to the actual physical skill. As the technique becomes more proficient, the neural pattern becomes stronger, and myelination of the associated axons become thicker.

Is there scientific evidence for soft and hard wiring as a neural learning basis? Although this area is still being explored, research has been under way since the mid-1960's. In 1966, J. V. McConnell was able to demonstrate that ribonucleic acid (RNA) is, in fact, involved in the learning process by transferring RNA from one rat to another. In 1970, George Ungar followed McConnell's research and was able to transfer a protein from the brain of a rat who was afraid of the dark, to another rat who subsequently became afraid of the dark. Additional studies have identified "a recent series of experiments indicates that short-term memory involves a primarily electrical activity in the brain, and long-term memory predominantly involves a chemical process, and the possible modification of proteins. . . Researchers Flood and Jarvik have reported that drugs which affect the synthesis of the proteins or their transfer along the axons, only affect long-term memory; whereas drugs that affect electrical activity in the brain only affect short-term memory" (Rose, 1985).

Making the transition from soft wiring to hard wiring is a process of technique refinement. As the students begin to practice a skill, the survival motor program in the form of soft wiring will provide the basis of the skill's performance. As the students practice the initial twenty-five repetitions, the transition to hard wiring will be influenced by several variables, such as personal feedback, instructor feedback, and the knowledge of the practice results. Since achieving technique confidence in a short period of time is critical, feedback is the most important aspect of beginning practice sessions. Cognitive processing, therefore, should be the instructor's primary focus.

Hard wiring a survival motor program quickly will be a result of the instructor's presentation of a skill and the method of practice endorsed. The author suggests teaching a skill in three components. In other words, breakdown the technique into three major components, and do not allow the students to proceed to step two until step one has been performed at an acceptable level. This allows the students to fully concentrate on mastering each skill component without the distractions of trying to learn the other components.

Next, the instructor should provide all verbal feedback in small portions. When feedback is focused on a specific technique flaw instead of several technique flaws, the students can concentrate and refine that portion of the survival motor program. In conjunction with this principle, all feedback (verbal or visual) should be very specific in correcting a single technique flaw and creating a corrected mental picture for the student. Remember, the purpose of all instructor feedback is to correct the neural patterns of a survival program. This can only be accomplished by making the students consciously understand what was done incorrectly and then providing a correct picture to model.

Stimulus/Condition Response Training Principle

All too often survival instructors spend a majority of their training on refining the survival response to be used in the field. In fact, many instructors believe that for students to perform a skill in the field under combat stress, the students must perform several thousand repetitions in training. Although this is a critical aspect of training, we must not forget that survival and combat training consists of two elements. The first is threat recognition, and the second is response selection to a specific threat. The second element, response selection, is as critical to a student's survival as being able to perform a survival skill competently.

Training the students to perform a skill in the stress of combat goes beyond teaching a series of skills. When the students face a threat in the field, they will process the threat and react methodically. The process begins with the identification and analysis of the level of threat or resistance. The subconscious will then select a response which is based upon past training and experiences. Subsequently, the survival motor program will be downloaded into the central nervous system, resulting in a specific muscle/motor response. This reaction time process occurs every time the students must respond to any type of threat stimulus.

The key to successful survival training is finding methods to decrease the student's reaction time to a threat stimulus, and provide training which will condition the students to an automatic response without hesitation. This cannot occur through static skill repetition, in which the skill is not practiced without the threat stimulus. Static skill repetition does nothing to program students to perform a skill in the stress of a field application. An automatic response to a specific threat can only occur when the students practice a skill in conjunction with a specific level of threat. This is known as the Stimulus/Condition Response Training Principle. This principle is based upon the interaction which occurs during a conditioned response, such as the flinching of a hand away from a hot object (the stimulus).

The principle is based on the association of all neural patterns. Specific motor skills are triggered by stimuli through daily associations. Recall and automatic responses are not the result of high training repetitions. For a response to be a conditioned or an automatic response, there must be an associated stimulus which triggers the response. Therefore, if a survival motor program is expected to be automatic to a threat in the field, the two must be combined early in the student's training. Since myelination increases with repetition, and all new experiences ultimately form a motor program, the logic of quick recognition and recall of a motor program appear to based upon repetition of the stimulus and the survival motor program.

Chapter Two Summary

The research on the neural basis of memory reaches beyond current methods of survival skill instruction. The research findings clearly demonstrate that teaching a skill alone will not condition the student to respond to a threat stimulus. Instead, research indicates that the focus of our training should be directed at the development of automatic responses to a specific threat stimuli. This can be accomplished if instructors examine their training and coincide the skills learned with a stimulus, which simulates a threat stimulus that the student will meet in combat. The following chapters will examine this concept further and provide some insight into design methodologies.

Chapter Two References

Deporter, B. and Hernacki, M. (1992). *Quantum Learning*: Dell Publishing.

Hontz, Tom (1995). *Vertical Versus Horizontal Decision Making For Officer Survival Training*

Johnson, George (1991) *In The Palaces of Memory*: Vintage Books.

McConnell, J.V. (1966) As cited in *Accelerated Learning*, Dell Publishing

Millman, Dan (1979). *The Warrior Spirit, Mind Body and Spirit*: Stillpoint Publishing.

Moravec, Hans, (1992). *Minds With Mobility*, Discovery Magazine, (1992, November Issue).

Rose, Colin (1987). *Accelerated Learning*, Dell Publishing.

Schneider, A and Tarshis, B. (1986) *Physiological Psychology,* Random House

Unger, George (1970) As cited in *Accelerated Learning*, Dell Publishing

3

Survival Motor Skill Classification

"Advanced techniques are the basics mastered."

Author unknown

I n chapter one a theory was proposed which stated that one of the key elements to learning a skill quickly is to base all survival training upon simple motor skills. This theory suggested that technique simplicity not only affects the speed at which the student learns a skill, but will indirectly enhance the student's motivation to train longer.

Since the study of motor skill performance is directed at enhancing the student's ability, it is appropriate for survival instructors to examine the field of motor behavior and performance. This field has over a century of research that can assist survival instructors in the development of survival systems.

In essence, the ideal survival skill should be kept as simple as possible in technique complexity, technique response time, and theory of application.

Motor Skill Classifications

Survival skills instructors have the responsibility to provide students with techniques and tactics that may save the student's life or the life of another. A responsibility of this magnitude is not one that should be taken lightly. Virtually no other field empowers an individual with training designed to specifically take a human life. Subsequently, the survival skills instructor has an ethical and legal responsibility to provide his students with the best training possible.

As in the case of many professions, researching the environmental conditions and performance limitations are critical to the development of training. Therefore, survival skills must be designed around two key factors. The first is to develop techniques that can be quickly learned by an individual with average physical and mental capabilities. The second is to develop the understanding of the psychological stresses that accompany a survival situation.

Traditionally, survival training has been conducted in semi-static environments. Although static training does allow the student a safe environment to practice a skill, there are many conditions of survival stress that cannot be isolated or duplicated outside the real threat. Therefore, we cannot correctly assume that techniques which are successful in training, will also be effective in the field. However, some of the research findings in the field of motor skill behavior can help us explain why students will often fail to utilize their training. In fact, many technique failures may be a result of teaching skills that are not adaptable to survival stress.

The study of motor skill behavior was developed from the field of psychology. Sage (1984) defines the science of motor skill behavior, "As a field of study, it is an attempt to learn more about the psychological factors involved with motor learning, control, and performance. The primary concern of scientists working in this subject area is with the understanding and knowledge of human movement. Scientists studying motor behavior have a threefold purpose. First, they seek to understand the behavioral dimensions of human movement. The second purpose is explanation. As a result of understanding the subject matter, they want to be able to explain behavior. Their third purpose is prediction. As a result of understanding and having the ability to explain behavior, they want to be able to predict behavior."

Although research on motor control and learning is usually linked to the research of experimental psychologists, the study of motor skill behavior can be dated back to 1897. It was during this time that two researchers, Bryan and Harter, studied the skill acquisition and motor learning principles of Morse code. From the early 1900s to 1945, research in this field changed directions toward the industrial setting. However, motor skill behavior was applied to survival training for the first time during World War II. It was during this time that scientists, encouraged by large research grants from the government, began to examine the consequences of fine motor skill training on pilots. This period lasted from 1945 to the early 1960s.

The field of motor skill behavior took a giant step during the early 1960s, with the research of Franklin M. Henry. Henry was an experimental psychologist working in the Department of Physical Education at the University of California. His research was directed at studying gross motor skills in athletic events. He also pioneered research on the differences of performance among different sized athletes, practice schedules, the mathematical shapes of performance curves, and the role of fatigue in performance. It was Henry's graduate students who continued his research and created an interest in the motor behavior field, which also led to sports psychology.

As research continued on the affects of stress and motor skill performance, it became evident that stress (arousal) had a direct influence on the optimal performance levels of skills, using various muscle groups. Yerkes and Dodson were the first researchers to explore this issue in 1908. Their research, referred to as the **Yerkes-Dodson Law**, states that "optimal arousal for behavioral efficiency decreases with increased task difficulty or complexity" (Sage, 1984). However, their research also identified the problem of attempting to classify the level of task difficulty.

Throughout the years researchers have developed a number of motor skill classifications. The most common classifications include gross, fine, discrete, serial, continuous, open, and closed motor skills. However, it was Cratty who suggested that motor skills can be classified on a progressive continuum from fine to gross, "with a reference to size of the muscle involved, the amount of force applied, or to the magnitude of space in which the movement is carried out" (Sage, 1984). Cratty's research was just the beginning of several different studies that have classified motor skills according to muscle size, task complexity, fatigue, levels of stress, and increasing degrees of heart beats per minute. Although there are several different models of skill classification, the author has focused on Cratty's analysis because of the compatibility factor to survival training principles.

Gross motor skills are skills that generally involve the action of large or major muscle groups. Examples of a gross motor skill would be simple actions such as walking, jumping, swimming, or a squatting or pressing movement. Since gross motor skills utilize large muscle groups, they could also be referred to as strength events. For the purpose of studying survival skills, consider a gross motor skill as a pushing or pulling event, or any event which has double-appendage symmetry. As a strength event, a high level of arousal (motivation, excitement, or psyching-up) will increase the optimal performance level due to increased adrenal secretions.

Fine motor skills are skills performed by small muscle mass or groups, such as hands and fingers; and frequently involve hand-eye coordination. Actions such as typing, handwriting, or playing the piano would be considered fine motor skills. In the survival skill category, a fine motor skill would include any action that requires precision hand-eye coordination, such as shooting a firearm accurately.

Countless studies have found that to maintain optimal performance conditions for fine motor skills, the conditions should maintain at low or nonexistent stress levels. This seems especially true of skills that require a high degree of accuracy and cognition.

Complex motor skills are skills which involve hand-eye coordination, timing or tracking, and have multiple technique components. Complex motor skills will combine a series of individual muscle group actions to form a single event. Examples of this would include athletic events such as a quarterback throwing a football on the run for accuracy; or a baseball player faking a bunt to pull in the third baseman, and then taking a full swing at a pitch. Survival skills that would be considered complex motor skills include a shooting stance that has muscle groups working in different or asymmetrical movements, or a takedown that has more than three independent movements from different muscle groups.

As with the performance of fine motor skills, studies have indicated that the optimal performance conditions for complex motor skills is in a low-stress environment. Subsequently, British psychologist E. C. Poulton (1957) suggested that skills could be classified into categories that are based upon environmental events and conditions. Poulton also suggested that skills can be classified as either open or closed. This concept was later advanced by British physical educator Barbara Knapp (1961). Knapp identified the perceptual influences on open and closed motor skills.

Open motor skills are skills that are conducted in a dynamic environment and should be considered reactionary motor skills. An example would be an actual combat shooting in which an officer would have to react to the deadly-force actions of the assailant. In this situation, the officer must not only find cover, obtain target acquisition on the assailant, and return fire, but he must also handle the stress of another individual attempting to kill him.

Closed motor skills are skills conducted in a static, non-stressful environment. A static environment could be identified as an environment which is stable and consistent. An example would include a firearms qualification in which the student performs the firing sequences on command at targets that are consistently the same and do not shoot back.

The Affects of Stress on Performance: The Inverted-U Hypothesis

The literature on motor skill behavior does identify and address the affects of stress, or arousal, on the performance of each motor skill classification. From 1900 through the 1940's, studies on the effects of effort and performance found that induced arousal facilitated the performance of cognitive activities. (Arousal is the scientific term used to describe various levels of stress. For the purposes of this text, the term "stress" will be used to identify survival stress.) Studies also found that performance would not equally benefit from increased stress; and in fact, that performance deteriorated as stress increased through intermediate levels.

The study of the affects of stress on performance led to the development of the **Inverted-U Hypothesis**. "The Inverted-U Hypothesis simply proposes that increases in arousal are accompanied in the quality of performance up to a certain point, after which additional increases in arousal result in a deterioration in the quality of performance" (Sage 1984).

Sage successfully classifies skills into several different categories that help put the research into proper perspective for survival training. He classifies task complexity by perceptual and cognitive demands, the terms of the degree of inhibition and precision required, and the complexity of the task movement.

The issue of complexity by perceptual and cognitive demands was explored by Weinberg and Hunt (1973). They found that high or even moderate levels of stress appear to interfere with fine muscular control and decision making. The study stated that complex cognitive skills degrade with even slight increases in stress. In contrast, motor skills dominated by large muscle groups which have minimal fine motor control and very little decision making or cognitive complexity, were not affected by high levels of stress. Schmidt (1991) observes, "If skills require very fine muscular control (as in archery) or have important decision making components (as in being a quarterback), then the point of maximum arousal is generally shifted to the left of the inverted curve."

The performance curve referred to by Schmidt is a method of measuring the performance of a skill in relation to relative levels of stress. For fine motor skills, or motor skills which have a high degree of cognitive decision making, the research indicates that optimal performance will occur during low levels of stress. Motor skills that are moderate in motor control and cognitive complexity will produce best results during moderate levels of stress. Motor skills that use large muscle mass (gross motor skills) and are cognitively simple (require very little decision making) produce optimal performance during high levels of stress.

From a physiological perspective, this principle is quite reasonable. We know that when the human body perceives stress, the body increases the production of adrenal hormones. The adrenal hormones increase blood supply to the extremities, thus increasing an individual's strength potential. This explains why gross motor skills, such as power-lifting, can be performed optimally under high levels of stress. However, an increase in adrenal hormones will also interfere with fine motor skills and accuracy during event performance.

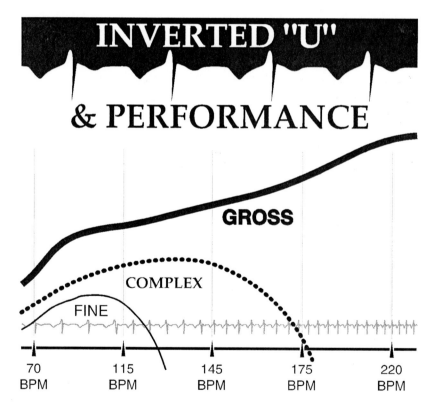

These observations have been the subject of several studies on the Inverted-U Hypothesis. Shelton and Mahoney (1978) studied the affects "psyching-up" has on the performance of weight lifters. They had one group lower their stress levels by either counting backwards or by squeezing a hand dynamometer. The second group was allowed to psych-up for the strength event. They found that the group which was instructed to psych-up showed tremendous improvement, while the first group had virtually no improvement at all.

A similar study by Weinberg, Gould, and Jackson (1979) found that the effects of psyching-up were task-specific. Their research indicated that psyching-up helped increase simple dynamic strength events but had no effect on balance or speed of arm movement events.

Several different studies have examined the affects of physical stress on performance. Exercise-induced activation experiments (EIA) use exercise to increase the resting heart rate of subjects while monitoring their performance with different types of motor skills. Levitt and Gutin (1971) studied the performance of a five-choice reaction time task and found that the ideal resting heart rate performance is at the rate of 115 heart beats per minute. This rate is interpreted by researchers as being a low to moderate level of stress. After the heart rate increased above 115 beats per minute, the subject's performance began to deteriorate, with the worst performance at 175 beats per minute.

Similarly, Levitt (1972) examined the affects of various stress levels induced by exercise, on tasks varying information-processing demands. Levitt measured his students' responses by recording their heart rates at intervals of 80, 115, 145, and 175 beats per minute. He found a clear Inverted-U effect, with optimal performance at the heart rate of 115 to 145 beats per minute. His students' performances were clearly less effective at heart beats of 80 and 175 beats per minute.

The study of the Inverted-U Hypothesis has led researchers to examine not only the muscle groups involved in a skill, but also the cognitive processes associated with the skill. Sage (1984) stated that, "motor tasks requiring concentration, judgment, discrimination, and fine muscle control, such as in tracking, aiming, and steadiness, are performed best under rather low to moderate states of arousal. Conversely, motor tasks demanding strength, endurance, speed, or those in which ballistic movements dominate, necessitate rather high levels of arousal."

Although the research on motor behavior and performance is extensive, the research on survival training has been minimal. However, two studies are consistent with the existing body of research and school of thought. The first study examined the use of the combat shooting stance under stress. Currently there are two different schools of thought on shooting stances in the United States.

The first, and oldest, is that of the Isosceles shooting stance, which is a crouched shooting stance that squares-off on the target. The stance usually finds the shooter with his feet slightly wider than shoulder width, arms stretched straight out toward the target, and gun at eye level. The Isosceles stance is also referred to as the instinctive crouch. The second predominant stance is the Weaver shooting stance, developed by Jack Weaver in 1958. The Weaver stance places the shooter in a three-quarter side stance, with the dominant arm almost straight and the support arm bent approximately at a 45 degree angle. Weaver proponents state that this stance is biomechanically stronger than the Isosceles stance. The Isosceles advocates believe their stance is more instinctive and more natural to learn.

Westmoreland (1989) was first to examine which stance was more suitable for the affects of combat stress. His study examined ninety-eight shooting scenarios that were either spontaneous or non-spontaneous in nature. The majority of the participants were Weaver advocates and proclaimed to be Weaver practitioners. To enhance stress, the participants used ammunition that had been modified to shoot cotton projectiles. The results of Westmoreland's research is as follows:

Spontaneous under 10 feet: 39 total scenarios
    96.7 % Isosceles   (29 events)
     3.3 % Weaver   (1 event)
    62.1 % One-handed stance (Isosceles) (18 events)
    23.1 % Failed to respond   (9 events)

Spontaneous over 10 feet: 27 total scenarios
    92.6 % Isosceles   (25 events)
     7.4 % Weaver   (2 events)
    14.8 % One-handed stance (Isosceles) (4 events)
Non-Spontaneous under 10 feet: 27 total scenarios

74.1 % Isosceles	(20 events)
25.9 % Weaver	(7 events)

Non-Spontaneous over 10 feet: 5 total scenarios
     60.0 % Isosceles   (3 events)
     40.0 % Weaver   (2 events)

Study Totals
     56.1 % Two-handed Isosceles stance   (55 events)
     12.2 % One-handed Isosceles stance   (12 events)
     22.5 % Two-handed Weaver stance   (22 events)
     9.2 % Of the officers failed to respond   (9 events)

The results of this study appear to concur with the current body of literature in motor behavior research. Westmoreland identified several factors that he believes led to the research findings. First, he identifies the issue of motor skill classification for each stance. Westmoreland identifies the Weaver stance as a fine motor skill based upon the use of small muscles of the hand, hand-eye coordination, and needed precision.

After studying the results of Westmoreland's research, an argument can be made that the Weaver stance is not a fine motor skill, but a complex motor skill. If we were to list the separate components of the Weaver stance, they would be as follows:

- The fine motor skills of hand-eye coordination.
- Precision in target engagement.
- Asymmetrical positioning of the upper body, as compared to the lower body.
- Asymmetrical actions of the arms.

- Applying the push/pull isometric action of the grip.
- Canting the head at an angle to acquire the proper sight picture.
- Canting the body in a side stance to the target.

In contrast, the Isosceles stance is considerably more simple to execute. It advocates squaring-off on the target, symmetrical positioning of the arms, and symmetrical positioning of the legs. Although we still must add the fine motor skill action of hand-eye coordination, we have a stance that is a more natural action and much more simple to execute in high-stress situations.

Westmoreland also identified the "sudden injection of stress," which he links to the history of both stances. Westmoreland traced the inception of the Isosceles stance back to 1927 in Shanghai. At that time, Fairbairn and Sykes identified that men in a firefight would assume an "instinctive crouch," with both arms stretched in front of them to obtain a natural targeting system, (Westmoreland,1989). The key consideration is that the stance was designed by observing the actions of men during the stress of combat or in an open motor skill environment.

It is reported that in 1958, Jack Weaver developed the Weaver stance to enhance his speed and accuracy during shooting competitions. (This is disputed by most firearms researchers who stipulate that the current Weaver stance was actually developed by John Henry Fitzgerald in 1930. An excellent reference on this topic is *Quick or Dead*, authored by William Cassidy.) Unlike a firefight, a firearms competition is a closed motor skill in which the environment is always the same. Additionally, the practitioner never has to react to another individual's hostility.

The last element evaluated by Westmoreland is the issue of "an inborn reflex to squarely face the attack." Westmoreland comments on the fight or flight syndrome: "That response, when suddenly attacked especially in close quarters, is to face our opponent squarely with our hands and arms extended out in front of us. This a natural stance assumed by all animals who defend themselves on two legs. Add a handgun and you have an Isosceles stance." Westmoreland's research was reviewed and supported by several different sports psychologists.

The first, Robert Weinberg (1988), stated, "From my experience as a researcher in the area of stress and psychomotor performance, I offer the following thoughts. One principle that seems appropriate is that individuals usually return to their preferred or instinctive mode of behavior (in this case, a movement pattern), especially under stress. When put into a stressful situation (in a police officer's job, sometimes life threatening), it is instinctual to face your opposition rather than turn to the side. This is a strong instinct since it is part of the fight or flight response to danger." Tom Seabourne wrote, "The 'front stance' (Isosceles) may simply be more comfortable to the officer even though prior training dictated the Weaver style. The 'front stance' may feel stronger to the officer as both hands are applying equal force. There may simply be an inherent flaw in the Weaver approach."

The concept of an "inborn reflex" is an issue that we cannot overlook. Westmoreland made a strong argument that survival training should be developed from natural responses to critical situations. The Isosceles stance was designed from such methodology. The Weaver stance, however, was not designed for combat purposes, but for competition shooting in which the shooter is not under the stress of survival. The Isosceles stance was designed from an open motor skill environment for the open motor skill environment of actual combat. The Weaver stance was designed to increase performance in a closed skill environment and later, tried to make the transition to an open skill environment.

The second study examining survival training issues, reviewed the technique preference of officers who had been trained in the side handle baton. Garcia (1989) surveyed approximately 400 police officers who had been trained in side handle baton systems, which advocate teaching over thirty techniques. His study examined which techniques were most commonly used, why some techniques were favored over others, and the apparent lack of research validation in baton system development.

To obtain needed information, Garcia developed a questionnaire that was divided into two sections. The first section listed the most common twenty-seven side handle baton techniques currently used by several different systems. He asked the participants of the study to identify the number of times they had used each technique by using the following format:

a. 0 - never used
b. 1 - used one time
c. 2 - used two times
d. 3 - used three times or more

The respondent would then circle the correct number of technique applications he had previously used during a field arrest. The results of the questionnaire are as follows:

Technique	Reported Uses	% of Totals
Spins	794	34.5 %
Jabs	562	24.4 %
Chops	296	12.9 %
Basic blocks	182	7.9 %
Power blocks	113	4.9 %
Armlocks	238	10.4 %
Hooking techniques	114	5.0 %

Like Westmoreland, Garcia also found that complex motor skills were rarely used. The side handle baton techniques (which could be categorized as gross motor skills such as spins, jabs, chops, and basic blocks) were used in over 79.7% of the situations. Techniques that would be considered a complex motor skill (power blocks, arm locks, and hooking techniques) were used in 20.3% of the situations.

On the second section of the questionnaire, Garcia asked a series of questions regarding the officer's most recent application of a side handle baton technique, as well as several questions on training and technique confidence. Garcia found that, "When asked which techniques they felt least confident using, most respondents (189) listed hooking techniques. The reasons given for this lack of confidence included, 'need more training', 'lack of practice', 'too complicated', 'too much movement', and that the technique 'cannot be practiced alone'. When asked which techniques they were most confident in using, the majority of respondents (226) chose spinning techniques. The reasons given included, 'easy to remember', 'simple', and the technique 'feels more natural'."

Garcia concluded his study with, "The results of this research are self-evident. Police officers will not use something they are not comfortable with. They have no confidence in the hooking techniques, and they are not using them. The same can be said for the blocking techniques (both basic and power). Certainly the overwhelming majority of officers using the baton are using it in some sort of striking manner (spins and jabs). Respondents felt that these techniques were the easiest and most effective among those taught in the basic course. As the techniques became more complicated, or less effective, the use began to taper-off dramatically. Armed with this information, defensive tactics and baton instruction must offer techniques which are easily practiced and mastered by the officer, while at the same time provide the needed skills to defend him/herself or others. Given the very real time and economic constraints placed on training, it simply does not make sense to teach skills that are not going to be used."

Westmoreland provided sound theory to support his "inborn reflex" concept, basing his theory on the fact that gross motor skills are naturally more easy to perform during high-stress situations. Garcia not only supported Westmoreland's theory, but advanced the theory by adding the perspective of "perceived capabilities." Garcia found that the respondents favored techniques that "appeared to be simple to perform without the need for extensive practice." He also identified the issue of favoring techniques which the officer could practice alone. But once again, the techniques which can be practiced alone are gross motor skills.

Chapter Three Summary

The advancement of any science can always be associated with the development of related principles. As researchers gain insight on the fundamental principles of the science, they can then establish basic laws that will apply to that specific science. In the case of the science of survival training, we can develop some basic fundamental laws by combining the survival research and the existing research on motor skill behavior. Considerations would be as follows:

• The research clearly indicates that fine and complex motor skills begin to deteriorate when the working heart rate accelerates beyond 145 beats per minute. This is especially true of hand-eye coordination skills and aiming events. (This will be examined further in the following chapters.) Since it is reasonable to expect any survival situation to increase the student's heart rate beyond 145 beats per minute, all survival training should be based on gross motor skills whenever possible.

• All techniques should be designed for maximum certainty of success, with a minimal outlay of physical or mental energy.

•   A portion of all survival training should be directed at simulation training to provide a base of experiences relating to the survival skill. This will accomplish two goals. First, the simulation will associate a survival skill with a predicted assault, thus making reaction time quicker. Second, simulation training, when correctly administered, will reduce the student's anxiety and working heart rate levels by giving him an experience relating to a skill's field application. This develops the student's confidence in a skill, which in turn lowers working heart rates.

•   The research indicates that optimal motor skill performance and cognitive processing occur at working heart rates within a zone of 115 to 145 beats per minute. Subsequently, training students to understand that they have an ideal survival performance heart rate could help them during a survival situation.

Finally, if the survival skills are based upon gross motor skills, the technique should not require a great deal of cognitive processing, resulting in faster student learning and higher training motivation. Higher motivation leads to longer practice periods, which in turn develops higher skill. The cycle will then start again. If survival training is to evolve into a science, the techniques and systems must be based upon research. The findings on existing motor skill behavior and survival literature validates the concept of simplicity, which is several thousand years old. It stands to reason that technique and system simplicity should be a foundation of all aspects of survival training.

Chapter Three References

Bryan, W.L. and Harter, N. (1899) *Studies in the Physiology and Psychology of Telegraphic Language.* Psychological Review, 4, 27-53.

Cassidy, W. L., (1978). *Quick or Dead;* Boulder Paladin Press.

Cratty, B. J. (1973). *Movement Behavior and Motor Learning.*

Garcia, R. (1989). *A Field Study of Side Handle Baton Techniques;* PPCT Research Publications.

Guthrie, E. R. (1952) *The Psychology of Learning,* Harper & Row.

Knapp, B. N. (1961). *A Note on Skill,* Occupation Psychology 35.

Levitt, S. and Gutin, B. (1971) *Multiple Choice Reaction Time and Movement Time During Physical Exertion,* Research Quarterly 42.

Levitt, S. (1972) *The Effects of Exercise Induced Activation Upon Simple, Two-Choice and Five-Choice Reaction Time and Movement Time.* Doctoral Dissertation.

Poulton, E. C. (1957). *On Prediction in Skilled Movements,* Psychological Bulletin 54.

Sage, G. H. (1984). *Motor Learning and Control; A Neural Psychological Approach,* William C. Brown Publishers.

Schmidt, R. A. (1991) *Motor Learning & Performance; From Principles to Practice,* Human Kinetics.

Shelton, T.O. and Mahoney, M.J. (1978) *The Content and Effect of Psyching-Up Strategies in Weight Lifters,* Cognitive Therapy & Research -2 (1979)

Weinberg, R.S.; Gould, D. & Jackson, A., *Expectations and Performance: An Empirical Test of Bandura's Self-Efficacy Theory.* Journal of Sport Psychology.

Westmoreland, H. (1989). *An Examination of Stress Shooting Stances;* PPCT Research Publications.

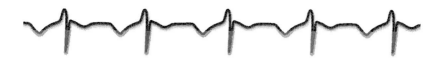

4

Survival Reaction Time

"Strategy is the science of making use of space and time. I am more jealous of the latter than the former. We can always recover lost ground, but never lost time."

Field Marshal August Graf von Gneisenau, 1761-1831

Time is a critical component of survival. When a student has the advantage of time, he can prepare and plan with clarity of mind. The stress level is in control, and the ability to scan for a threat stimulus is enhanced.

In contrast, "lost time" in a survival encounter initiates a chain reaction of escalating stress. As the stress increases, the student's heart rate increases. The ability to perform complex or fine motor skills immediately deteriorates. Perceptual narrowing occurs, slowing the information processing. Response programming is delayed until the threat level can be identified. Heart rates continue to increase as the student recognizes that the loss of time is increasing. Finally, a survival stress response occurs resulting in a desperate irrational response: fight, flight, or freezing in place (hypervigilance).

Training students in methods which minimize the affects of stress should be a priority of survival instructors.

Reaction time research and the subsequent laws have a profound affect on performance, which transcends individual skill. In fact, it could be argued that the study of reaction time principles may be one of the critical aspects of survival training. However, we must also recognize that enhancing reaction time crosses several different psychological and physiological components. Factors such as visual perception, mental alertness, training, life experiences, and stress levels will affect reaction time.

Reaction Time Defined

The study of reaction time principles has been a field of study dating back to the Civil War. Early studies on reaction time were conducted with crude electrical equipment to measure the delays in response to lights. Today, scientists have the benefit of advanced technology which helped us gain new insight on the cognitive processes of reaction.

We know that responding to any stimulus is a combination of cognitive processing and neural motor programs based upon perceptions and experiences. For decades scientists have recognized the multiple stages involved with a simple response to a stimulus. Subsequently, motor control scientists have developed clear terminology which represents each stage of a reactionary response. The terms which are most applicable to this chapter are *reaction time, movement time and response time.*

True *reaction time* is a function which occurs between the sensory nervous system and the brain's ability to recognize and identify a proper response to the threat; then download a motor program to the motor nervous system. Schmidt (1988) defines reaction time as "a measure of time from the arrival of a suddenly presented and unanticipated signal to the beginning of the response to it." Therefore, reaction time by definition is a pure cognitive task.

The second stage is *movement time*, which is normally defined as the time from the interval between the beginning and the end of the movement. In the case of survival training, movement time would be identified as the length of time a specific survival skill would take to complete.

The third stage is *Response Time*. This is the combination of reaction time and movement time. It would be defined as the length of time from the perception of the threat stimulus to the completion of the student's response.

Reaction Time and Information Processing Models

The study of reaction time would not be complete without reviewing the theories of information processing. Since reaction time by definition is a cognitive process involved in identifying and programming proper responses, the study of information processing is a major component in the stages of reaction time. For example, Pargman (1986) defines information processing as "the term used to refer to the deposition of information in memory, the retrieval of information from memory and the enactment of movement in response to a stimulus". This definition could easily be construed as a simple definition of reaction time.

Models depicting the processing of information are almost one hundred years old. Early models described information processing in three basic stages of Stimulus Presentation, Stimulus Identification and a Motor Response.

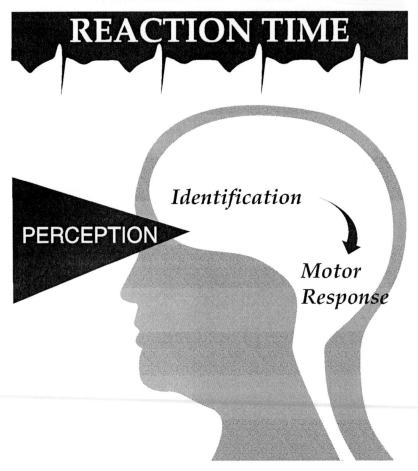

More recently, scientists have become increasingly interested in identifying the stages in more detail. This is largely due to the increases in technology which can scan the human brain and nervous systems. Through technology, scientists now generally separate information processing into the four stages of: perception, identification, selection and initiation.

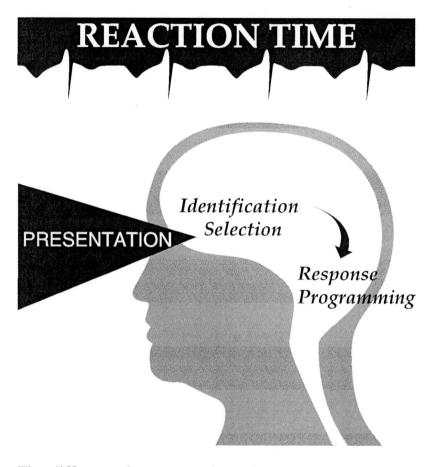

The difference between early and current models is the degree to which the brain can process and respond to a stimulus. The primary difference between the two models just examined is the brain's ability to identify, develop the appropriate motor response and then download this response to the motor nervous system within milliseconds.

Studying reaction time and information processing is not a recent phenomenon among survival instructors. W. E. Fairbairn of the Shanghai Police Department recognized the importance of survival reaction time when he developed the first true combat shooting house in 1917. Col. Rex Applegate (1943) in *Kill or Get Killed* discusses the need for quick shooting systems extensively. However, the first true examination of reaction time (limited to the author's research) is that of Ed McGivern.

In the 1930s, McGivern authored the text *Fast and Fancy Shooting*, where he attempted to examine the components of quick and accurate shot placement from a scientific perspective. His research provides an in-depth analysis of reaction time from a psychological perspective. He states;

> "Voluntary action, under normal conditions; an idea works itself out in action in the same way and to the degree to which it is the exclusive object of individual attention. But usually more than one idea is present in consciousness at the same moment, each striving, so to speak, to bring out its appropriate action. Action is thus delayed by the presence of competing ideas, causing what we call deliberation, reflection and choice. We reflect, we deliberate, we choose . . .
>
> The survivors of the many famous gun battles of that period were the ones who had their impulses and movements always under perfect control; no disturbing influence was great enough to throw them out of normal balance, no danger no matter how great or close, interfered with their positive movements, properly controlled, correctly timed, and accurately directed.

With such men it was not a case of lack of nerves as some try to make it appear; it was a matter of having everything in the way of impulse and emotions absolutely under control at the psychological moment, as the ones who are versed in such things generally refer to it.

Doctors and surgeons and professors, generally interested and well informed in such things, can and often do, explain clearly about man's reaction to what is termed 'the external stimulus to act.' These things are carried out in detail in the definitions of 'psychological time' and 'reaction time' under the branch of psychophysics; in short, it is the time elapsing between the application of a stimulus and the reaction to it, occasionally called psychophysical time. . .

Psychophysical time consists of three periods: First, a period of initial excitation of the sense organ and transmission of the stimulation to the third ganglionic center; second, a period of activity in the center; and, third, the period of the transmission of the motor impulse and of the physical reaction. The first and third of these constitute the 'psychological time.' The simple 'reaction time' is as nearly as possible, made identical with the 'psychological time,' the period of central activity being reduced to a minimum.

'Complex reaction times' are determinations of various sorts of central time. The usual types are: recognition, perception or discrimination time; choice time; and association time."

The depth of McGivern's analysis and insight is remarkable considering the time period. McGivern not only demonstrated an advanced understanding of reaction time fundamentals, but also appears to be one of the first researchers to apply reaction time principles to survival training. Ironically, the evolution of survival reaction time models has changed little over the last half century.

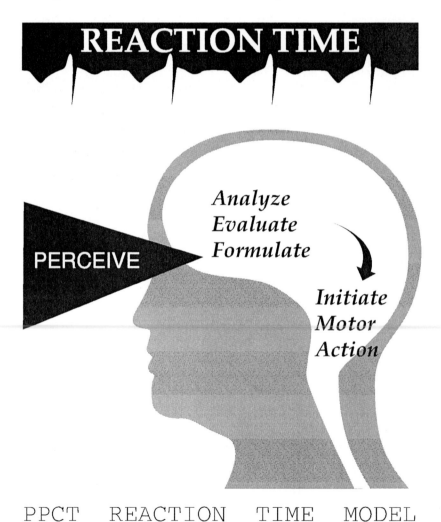

PPCT REACTION TIME MODEL

In 1982, the author introduced a survival reaction time model consisting of five stages. The model separates reaction time into the stages of Perception, Analysis/Evaluation, Formulate a Strategy and Motor Initiation.

The survival reaction time model advances McGivern's theory of cross analysis. This model suggests that reaction time is largely dependent upon the interaction of the analysis and evaluation of the stimulus. As the stimulus is perceived through the perceptual senses, the brain first analyzes or identifies the threat stimulus. If the threat is identified, the brain then evaluates additional variables which will determine the level of the threat. For example, a weapon found in an empty room would constitute a low level of threat. But if a student entered a room and found a subject standing over a body with a smoking gun in hand, the threat would be high.

The strategy formulation stage begins once the stimulus has been identified and evaluated. This stage will largely be dependent upon the combined perceptions of the previous two steps. The strategy will be formulated based upon several factors, such as the student's past training, the method of training and the number of similar experiences.

Once a strategy has been developed, the survival motor program will then be downloaded into the central nervous system and motor/muscle initiation occurs. The efficiency of the survival response will depend largely on the development of the survival motor program and the student's physical conditioning.

Beyond the terminology, the survival reaction time model differs little from contemporary reaction time models. However, the purpose of this model is to examine reaction time when a threat stimulus is present. This model places a heavy emphasis on the interaction between the analysis and evaluation stages. The author contends that analysis in of itself, is actually a single stage of identification. Evaluation is a component of the analysis stage, but is separate and can not occur until after the threat stimulus has been identified.

The benefits of this model center around two instructional objectives critical to survival training: why reaction time stalls and how to enhance reaction time. The term "mental stalls" was developed to identify how reaction time can breakdown at any one of the four stages of the survival reaction time model. For example, there can be a stall at the perception stage if the student is not paying attention and does not perceive (see) the threat. A stall occurs at the analysis stage if the student cannot identify the threat, or in the evaluation stage if the student misinterprets the level of threat. Finally, a stall may occur if the student does not have the proper training or experience to develop a strategy to counter the threat. If there is hesitation at any one of these stages, then the reaction time sequence is broken.

Preventing mental stalls is a matter of developing pre-planned strategies, a process loosely referred to as preprogramming. Preprogramming is based upon the premise that predicting and pre-planning a response will reduce reaction time. Studies by various motor skill researchers have found that reaction time may be reduced substantially, ranging from 150 milliseconds to 20 milliseconds (approximate).

Preprogramming appears to circumvent the strategy formulation stage and directly downloads the motor program into the central nervous system. The benefits of preprogramming are a substantial saving in a survival encounter where a millisecond could be the difference between life and death.

Memory Frameworks

An examination of reaction time models would not be complete without reviewing the theories of information processing and memory retrieval. We must remember that survival reaction time is the process of perceiving a survival threat and programming the appropriate survival response. Therefore, enhancing a student's reaction time is a matter of increasing the process of perceiving a threat and initiating a survival motor program.

Advancing the conceptual basis of reaction time and information processing is the theory of memory frameworks. This model proposes that information is processed through the three stages of memory called the Short Term Sensory Store, Short Term Memory, and the Long Term Memory.

The model holds that a stimulus is brought through the sensory nervous system (perceptual senses) to what is referred to as the Short Term Sensory Store (STSS). The STSS holds a picture of the stimulus for a short period of time estimated between 5-15 seconds based upon the intensity of the stimulus. The stimulus is then examined by the Short Term Memory.

The Short Term Memory (STM) is considered the working/thinking portion of the brain which is in a constant state of scanning information in the STSS. The STM analyzes the stimulus and then cross references (evaluates) the stimulus to the relevance for the moment. Based upon the results of the analyzing and evaluation, the STM will develop a motor program that is best suited for the stimulus.

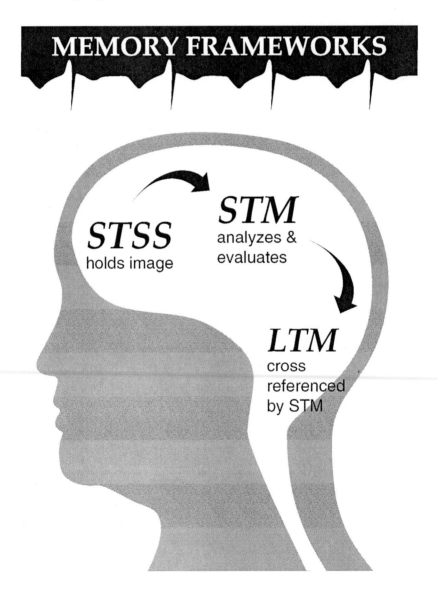

MEMORY FRAMEWORKS

STSS
holds image

STM
analyzes &
evaluates

LTM
cross
referenced
by STM

In the event the STM does not immediately have an automatic response, the STM will search the Long Term Memory (LTM), which acts as the brain's computer storage banks. If the LTM can find the appropriate response, the response will be downloaded to the motor nervous system to initiate a motor action.

The theory of memory frameworks has many applications for the survival instructor. For example, once students understand the interaction of the three phases of information processing, they will have a "picture" and not an abstract concept of reaction time. As we explored in chapter one, teaching in pictures is critical to learning skills quickly.

Memory frameworks also provide us with another perspective of how information is processed and retrieved. For a moment, let us review how a threat stimulus and survival response is processed. A threat stimulus is perceived through the perceptual senses, keeping in mind that most threats will be processed through the visual system. A picture of this threat is brought to the Short Term Sensory Store where it is analyzed and evaluated by the Short Term Memory. If the Short Term Memory can immediately identify the threat and the appropriate survival response, a survival motor program is immediately downloaded into the central nervous system. However, if the Short Term Memory does not have an immediate response in storage, the Short Term Memory will access the Long Term Memory for a solution. Once the Long Term Memory has developed a solution to the threat, this information is transferred to the Short Term Memory and downloaded to the central nervous system.

The interaction between the perception of a threat and the downloading of the survival motor program provides a basis for reaction time. The longer the interaction is between any of the three stages, reaction time will proportionally increase. Therefore, the goal is to decrease the interaction between the three stages of memory, and preferably bypass the need to access Long Term Memory.

The role of Long Term Memory has been a confusing point to many instructors. The confusion has stemmed from the belief that storing information into Long Term Memory can only be acquired through thousands of techniques repetitions. This theory has no basis in the literature, and in fact, contradicts current thought on reducing reaction time.

Current theories on stages of memory stipulate that all information which is processed, is automatically stored in the Long Term Memory. Some researchers believe that once information is processed through the Short Term Memory, the information is immediately stored in Long Term Memory. Other researchers believe that information can bypass Short Term Memory completely. The true issue, however, is not the storage but the recall of information.

Survival reaction time requires that a student respond to a threat stimulus immediately. If the Short Term Memory must access the Long Term Memory, then reaction time increases substantially. Therefore, reducing reaction time is a matter of bypassing the need to access Long Term Memory through prediction and preprogramming a survival response.

Perception and Perceptional Narrowing

The deterioration of processing skills has long been noted in situations where survival stress is high. Activities such as irrational behavior, freezing in place, and failing to see or hear specific human activity is a common phenomena when survival stress is present. However, the research examining perceptual narrowing now provides instructors with a recognized and validated explanation. Perceptional narrowing includes the loss of the peripheral vision and the ability to continue to scan a large number of threat cues in times of high stress.

Easterbrook (1959) developed the cue-utilization theory which stipulates that when arousal and stress are low, the perceptual field is wide. However, as the amount of stress increases the perceptual field decreases and focuses on the most relevant cues. It appears that as selective attention focuses on the source of information that provides the most input regarding the threat, attention is directed away from information that is not considered relevant.

Schmidt (1991) describes this phenomenon using a search beam as an example. He states "As the level of arousal increases, the beam of the searchlight becomes more intense, more focused and narrow, which aids in the processing of those things which are actually illuminated. But at the same time, the narrowed beam eliminates some of the immediately adjacent cues that could be relevant to performance, and the increased distractibility (increases in the number shifts in the location of the beam) which often causes relevant sources of information to have attention taken way from them."

One study which measured response time in varying conditions of scuba diving was conducted in 1966 by Weltman and Egstrom. They measured the response time of divers to a light stimulus presented in the peripheral vision of the diver's masks. They found that as the test subjects moved from the static environment of the tank to the dynamic environment of the open ocean, response times increased up to 400%.

Explaining why the visual system narrows, can be explained through researching the effects of stress on the visual system. Sports Optometrist Hal Breedlove states that the visual system in high stress will have a major influence on how the brain and body react to a threat. Dr. Breedlove states that under stress, the visual system will narrow the field of focus on the specific threat. Under high stress, the pupils will dilate to gather more information and depth perception is diminished. The axillary muscle is inhibited which results in the inability to focus, creating blurred vision at greater distances. All combined, these physiological responses will have an immediate negative affect on reaction time. Since the brain is now receiving less information, reaction time and response times increase.

The perceptual narrowing research will often explain what appears to be irrational behavior. Such an example has developed in legal strategies in litigating criminal justice agencies when an officer's use of force did not seem reasonable. Examples would include negligent tactics and the use of force when innocent third parties are present.

Negligent tactics are often associated in situations where an officer's tactics necessitate the use of force. An example would be as follows: A officer is confronted with a weapon- yielding attacker who is irrational or suicidal. The subject moves toward the officer challenging and placing the officer's life in imminent danger. The officer retreats from the subject until the environment affords no more protection and the officer is forced to fire to protect his own or another's life.

Incredibly, agencies and officers have been litigated under the assumption that the officer used negligent tactics which necessitated the use of deadly force. However, Breedlove's research provides us with a scientific explanation based upon eye anatomy and the affects of stress on the visual system. When a student's working heart rate rises above 145 BPM, the visual system decreases the peripheral field and attention focuses on a threat stimulus. Since the brain is demanding more information to deal with the threat, the student will invariably retreat from the threat to widen the peripheral field.

Another example is the use of force with an apparent disregard for the safety of innocent third parties. These scenarios will often find an officer engaging in a firefight when innocent subjects are within close proximity. Negligence is proposed when the consequences of the officer's actions are tragic, even though his life or another is in immediate jeopardy.

The issue of "not seeing" third parties or missing relevant facts can be explained by Easterbrook's cue hypothesis theory and Schmidt's light beam analysis. Both theories are based upon the hypothesis that as attention increases on a single source for information, visual narrowing of the perceptual senses must occur to maximize input.

This corresponds with reports of tunnel vision or auditory exclusion in the stress of combat. Currently, we know the brain has at least five direct perceptual senses which provide feedback about the environment (sight, sound, smell, touch, taste). It has been theorized that the brain is in a constant state of switching from one or a combination of perceptual senses to provide feedback relevant to the moment.

In times of high stress, focusing becomes more intense to maximize critical information needed for survival. In fact, the perceptual narrowing can become so focused that information from the other senses is either discarded or turned off. Tunnel vision and auditory exclusion are by-products of this process, which explains why certain facts are missed in survival stress.

Processing Information and Stress
(Analysis and Evaluation)

Misinterpreting visual cues in the stress of survival is not an uncommon phenomena during survival stress. Police officers have often mis-identified objects as weapons during periods of high stress, leading to flawed judgement and sometimes tragic consequences.

Processing information could be argued as an extension of perception. The ability to analyze and evaluate information is just as critical to reaction time as "seeing" a threat. However, the affects of stress on processing information appear to be closely related to perceptual narrowing research findings.

Levitt (1972) examined the affects of various levels of stress on information and processing tasks. He was able to control the levels of stress by having the test subjects exercise on a treadmill and monitoring their working heart levels. He took readings at heart rates of 80, 115, 145 and 175, and found a clear Inverted-U with optimal performance when the heart rate level was between 115 and 145 beats per minute. Similarly, he found that poor performance was recorded when the heart rate was below 80 BPM and above 175 BPM. Under similar conditions, Levitt and Gutin (1971) found that a five choice RT was performed at optimal levels when the HR was around 115 BPM.

Why do processing skills deteriorate under similar conditions as perceptual processing? We must remember that processing skills (analysis and evaluation) are dependent upon perceptual input. If the perceptual input decreases, cognitive processing will automatically be effected. It appears that increased heart rates create a catastrophic affect on perceptual skills, cognitive processing skills, reaction time and motor skill performance.

A theory developed by Rene Thom (1975) could lead to an explanation. Thom's catastrophe theory is similar to the Inverted-U Hypothesis stating that performance will deteriorate when stress levels reach a certain point. However, the catastrophe theory states that catastrophic failure can be expected when high cognitive anxiety is combined with high levels of physiological arousal.

The differences between the Inverted-U and the catastrophe theories are minimal, yet substantial. The Inverted-U Hypothesis proposes that performance will gradually deteriorate as stress (arousal) increases. The catastrophe theory differs by citing a vertical deterioration in performance which is immediate. In other words, the bottom falls out.

The second difference is the causation of the performance. While the Inverted-U Hypothesis places the cause of deterioration on arousal or excitement, the catastrophe theory places an the emphasis on high cognitive anxiety and physiological stress (arousal) combined.

The combination of high anxiety and physiological stress lends to the environment of survival stress. Survival stress can be defined in many ways. However, the components of survival stress are intertwined between accelerated levels of mental and physical stress. The combination of both is hypothesized as the causation of catastrophic failure. However, we cannot discount the negative affects of mental stress alone.

Unlike the stress brought on by physical exertion, mental stress in the form of high anxiety such as fear, apprehension, anger or the sense of hopelessness can have the same negative affects on the heart rate. Medical texts cited hundreds of cases where sudden anxiety produces unusually high heart rates, ultimately leading to an irregular heartbeat and death.

Unfortunately, bad judgement is often a by-product of the body's adaptation to survival stress. First, as the heart rate increases, the visual system adjusts to deal with the threat limiting the amount of information the brain receives. Second, the brain's normal ability to process (analyze and evaluate) a wide range of information quickly is focused to specific items. Therefore, additional cues which would normally be processed are either lost or misinterpreted. If the stress is perceived as spontaneous and overwhelming, hypervigilance occurs.

Can perceptual narrowing and the degradation of processing skills be prevented through training? Possibly, but we must keep in mind that perceptual narrowing is a result of high stress. Any time the heart rate escalates in a life threatening situation or when we are confronted with sudden and unanticipated threat stimulus, perceptual narrowing *will occur*.

Formulating Strategies; Hick's Law

A critical element of survival training is designing systems which will enhance a student's reaction time under combat stress. We have already addressed the research which discusses the mechanics of processing limitations under stress. This research also applies to the ability to develop an appropriate response, when the STM is not prepared for the threat. However, survival instructors need to be cognitive of the system design and the number of response options taught to students.

There have always been two primary views on system design in survival training. One philosophy states that instructors should teach a large number of techniques. This theory advocates that the more response options a student has to face a threat, the better prepared he will be.

The second theory maintains a more simplistic approach of keeping the number of response options to a minimum. The proponents of this system focus on a small number of techniques which students can learn quickly and easily while developing skill and confidence. Although there are strong arguments for both philosophies, the effects of stress and reaction time on decision making processes suggest that keeping response options to a minimum are preferred.

A number of studies support this view, dating back to Merkel's 1885 study. Merkel's study found that reaction time increased approximately 35% when choice reaction time went from one to two stimuli.

Hick (1952) examined reaction time increases from the perspective of increasing the number of responses to a specific stimulus. He found that as the number of response options (techniques) increased from one to two, reaction time increased by 58%. Schmidt (1991) states that "Increased response latency due to a greater number of stimulus-response (S-R) alternatives is of critical importance in understanding skilled performances, forming the basis of Hick's Law. The increase in RT is very large when the number of alternatives is increased from one to two. . . RT might increase from about 190 milliseconds with simple RT to more than 300 ms for a two choice case — a 58% increase in the time required to process the stimulus information into the response." The significance of Hick's research has been established as a motor learning law referred as Hick's Law.

A 1993 examination of Hick's Law and survival reaction time was conducted by Joe Ferrera. Ferrera conducted a simple study measuring the reaction time of a single block to a punch at .183 milliseconds. When he increased the number of blocks (response options) to the strike from one to four, reaction time increased to .481 milliseconds.

Hick's research has strong implications for survival training. First, reaction time increases significantly because the STM must decide which response or technique is most appropriate for the threat. Even though the difference in time is in milliseconds, most instructors agree that a half second hesitation in a deadly force confrontation could be fatal.

Henry-Rogers Experiment

Another explanation for Hick's Law was a study conducted by Franklin Henry and Donald Rogers in 1960. They found that increases in reaction time are associated with the need to load a motor program. Henry and Rogers found that reaction time increased when;

- Additional elements or components in a series are added to the action.
- Anytime more than one limb must be coordinated.
- When the duration of a skill becomes longer.
- Anytime a movement becomes more complicated in any of the above ways, reaction time will increase because additional time is needed to organize and download the motor program.

The Henry-Rogers Experiment was unique for suggesting that reaction time will be partly based upon the complexity of the motor program. Their research found that the more complex the motor skill, the more reaction time can be expected to increase.

Chapter Four Summary

Simply put, the essence of survival reaction time is threat recognition and correct response selection. If we accept this statement as fact, then we must proceed in designing systems which encompass reaction time principles and laws.

Placing this chapter's research into perspective centers around understanding performance limitations. Traditional reaction time research is conducted in environments where the perception of personal threat is low or nonexistent. But even in these conditions, we find reaction time increases as the heart rate accelerates.

Survival reaction time has variables which are more extreme. Spontaneous survival stress has an almost immediate affect on the heart rate, and perceptual narrowing will be more pronounced. Once perceptual narrowing occurs, information processing slows, and response selection is delayed until the threat level can be fully identified and evaluated. This begins a negative spiral which leads to hypervigilance, incorrect response selections or a continuous feedback loop (such as continuing to squeeze a trigger even though the weapon has been emptied).

The author is convinced that controlling the heart rate is the answer to survival performance. All of the research exposed in this text suggests survival skills such as visual processing, cognitive processing and motor performance deteriorate under accelerated heart rates. This is the paradox. Optimal survival performance requires moderate heart rates. Yet, survival performance is conducted in an environment which is life threatening.

The complexity of spontaneous survival stress requires a holistic approach to training. The next chapter will begin to establish a training methodology that enhances survival reaction time and survival skill performance.

Chapter Four References

Applegate, R. (1943) *Kill or Get Killed*, Paladin Press

Cassidy, W. L., (1978). *Quick or Dead;* Boulder Paladin Press

Cratty, B. J. (1973). *Movement Behavior and Motor Learning,* Lea and Febiger

Easterbrook, J.A. (1959) *The Effects of Emotion on Cue-Utilization and the Organization of Behavior.* Psychological Review.

Garcia, R. (1989). *A Field Study of Side Handle Baton Techniques;* PPCT Research Publications

Guthrie, E. R. (1952) *The Psychology of Learning,* Harper & Row

Gutin, B. and Levitt, S. (1971). *Multiple Choice Reaction Time and Movement Time during Physical Exertion;* Research Quarterly

Knapp, B. N. (1961). *A Note on Skill,* Occupation Psychology 35

Levitt, S. (1972). *The Effects of Exercise Induced Activation Upon Simple, Two-Choice, and Five-Choice Reaction Time and Movement Time;* Doctoral Dissertation, Columbia University

McGivern, E. (1932 original) (1975, 1984) *Fast and Fancy Revolver Shooting;* New Win Publishing, Inc.

Pargman, (1986) *Stress and Motor Performance: Understanding and Coping,* Mouvment Publications.

Parsons, S. (1993) *Improving Short Term Memory Retention of Visual Short Term Sensory Store Stimulus;* PPCT Research Publications

Poulton, E. C. (1957). *On Prediction in Skilled Movements,* Psychological Bulletin 54

Sage, G. H. (1984). *Motor Learning and Control; A Neural Psychological Approach,* William C. Brown Publishers

Schmidt, R. A. (1991) *Motor Learning & Performance; From Principles to Practice,* Human Kinetics

Weltman, G. and Egstrom, G. H. (1966). *Human Factors*

5

Survival Stress Management

"It is our performance that grants us the respect of courage, not the lack of fear."

Paul Whitesell, Ph.D., 1989

O f the many variables affecting survival performance, the relationship between the perception of stress and accelerating heart rates is the most overlooked. The dynamics of this association explains why catastrophic failures occur in cognitive processing and motor performance, as well as the disparity in performance between the classroom and the field.

Unfortunately, this is the paradox of survival training. Unlike athletic events conducted in static environments, the execution of survival skills requires fast cognitive processing and the ability to perform a motor skill with a high degree of accuracy. However, when executed in response to a life threatening stimulus, performance will be inhibited by the immediate escalation of the heart.

Is this paradox resolvable? Yes, if we recognize that survival stress is a result of a life threatening perception.

Martens (1977) identified this connection when he defined stress as "the process that involves the perception of substantial imbalance between (environmental) demand and response capability, under conditions where the demand has important consequences."

Martens' definition focuses on several important issues. Specifically, he identifies threat perception, response capability, and the perception of time needed to manage the perception. If any one of these variables is out of balance, high anxiety develops and the heart rate immediately climbs. *The implications of this research are simple: students must be educated on the symptoms of survival stress and methods of controlling heart rates before survival performance deteriorates.*

Survival Stress Responses

The mechanism surrounding survival stress has been studied for almost a century. Current research has identified a process where the body automatically makes changes when exposed to a threat stimulus. The "fight or flight response" is a defense mechanism designed to prepare the body for an explosive survival reaction. Benson (1975) states that, "When we are faced with situations that require adjustment of our behavior, and involuntary response increases our blood pressure, heart rate, of breathing, blood flow to the muscles, and metabolism, preparing us for conflict or escape. When the fight or flight response is evoked, it brings into play the sympathetic nervous system, which is part of the autonomic, or involuntary, nervous system. The sympathetic nervous system acts by secreting specific hormones; adrenaline or epinephrine and noradrenaline, or norepinephrine. These hormones, epinephrine and its related substances, bring about physiologic changes of increased blood pressure, heart rate and body metabolism."

The results of the fight or flight response are dramatic. Blood flow is redirected to the major muscles (thighs, chest, arms) and away from the lower extremities. Although the major muscles are now primed for fight or flight, hand dexterity and coordination suffer from the vascular occlusion, resulting in deterioration of fine and complex motor skills.

Activation of the sympathetic nervous system also has an immediate affect on the visual system. During sympathetic response, the contour of the lens changes, affecting a number of survival skills. For example, visual tracking becomes difficult, the ability to focus on close objects (weapon sights or instruments) deteriorates and the peripheral field narrows (perceptual narrowing).

When any of these symptoms occurs, the amount of visual information about the threat stimulus is reduced. This leads to increases in reaction time, response time, and a heightened state of stress.

Hypervigilance

The most dangerous result of survival stress is a mental state called hypervigilance. Hypervigilance is often described as freezing in place and arises when a high level threat is perceived. Janis and Mann (1977) describe hypervigilance occurring when serious threats of physical injury of death are imminent and the time to manage the threat is short. Under these conditions individuals act impulsively and take actions which are later regretted. They found that hypervigilance "in its most extreme forms, consists of an extremely agitated state of panic or near-panic. It is characterized by indiscriminate attention to all sorts of minor and major threats cues as the person frantically searches for a means of escaping from the anticipated danger. Other salient characteristics of hypervigilance are temporary impairment of cognitive functioning and defective decision making . . ."

Whitesell (1989) carries this concept further. He states that when fear is present, "the visceral response is more intense and more quickly realized. The response is expedited by the fact that the cerebral cortex is bypassed to a large extent. The neuroendocrine system deals directly with the brain. . . For this reason, man—and animal, began to employ an automatic inhibition of the thinking process during the fear response. The primitive brain — the brain stem,— in a controlling sense shuts down the thinking cortex at the same time that it physically prepares the body for action."

The affects of high anxiety on performance mirror the findings of the last two chapters. For example, Janis, Defares, and Grossman (1983) report that when anxiety is high there is a "temporary loss of cognitive efficiency and a temporary loss of perceptual acuity, perceptual-motor coordination, and motor skills." The effects of high anxiety on motor performance are easy to understand. However, the affects of high anxiety on cognitive skills, may be linked to states of hypervigilance.

The manifestation of hypervigilance explains many of the bizarre actions taken by officers and soldiers in combat. Actions such as freezing in place, attempting irrational acts or repeating the same skill even though it is ineffective, are common when hypervigilance develops. Apparent criminal and civil actions of negligence can be explained by the fact the officer or soldier was under extreme levels of fear resulting from the threat stimulus or the assaulting subject.

Tactically, hypervigilance results from the perception of a threat and the student's lack of confidence in their ability to control the threat. The ramification of this insight is simple: stress is a matter of perception, and perceptions can be changed through the training process.

The association between increased heart rates and anxiety or fear is more often based upon the students' perception of control. "To have control is to have security. If they perceive mild danger, they become anxious. If they perceive intense danger, they become fearful. Used in this presentation, anxiety and fear are more the measure of 'intensity of perceived danger' than of separate entity. But a measure carries an individual signature. A stimulus that is fearful to one may be only anxiety provoking to another. . ." (Whitesell, 1989).

Design Methodologies for Survival Stress Management

There are many complexities associated with survival stress management. Issues such as student belief systems, past experiences, and fears will have a positive or negative influence on a student's perceptions of control. However, the level of survival stress is based upon three important perceptions: the perceived level of threat, the student's confidence in their ability to control the threat, and whether the exposure to the threat is a first time experience.

These perceptions are very critical to the design methodology of survival training. Ultimately, they should establish a foundation for the training goals and objectives. For example, hypervigilance research stipulates that anxiety increases when there is insufficient knowledge about pending stressful events. However, the basic function of goals and objectives is to inform the student why specific training is necessary. This concept follows the author's motivational theories on creating a need for the skill — which in the learning process — prepares the student for the unknown.

Developing confidence in training should be the primary goal of survival instructors. Confidence is a mindset based upon past experiences and observations. Therefore, creating confidence in survival skills is a two step process. The first step is developing confidence in a specific skill. The level of skill confidence will be affected by the speed of learning and the perceived effectiveness of the skill. The second step is developing situational confidence, where the student learns to apply the skill through dynamic training exercises (role playing).

The final perception which induces survival stress, is experience. The "experience factor" is often the most overlooked aspect of survival training. All too often, survival training never leaves the static environment. Students may learn the mechanics of the skill but they never learn how the skill will interact in an open or dynamic environment. As an example, consider the student learning water survival skills for the open ocean.

Learning to swim in the ocean is a motor skill requiring interaction with a constantly changing environment. When students first learn how to swim, they often learn the basic strokes in the shallow end of a pool. But when the student moves to deep water, instructors will notice an increase in anxiety, even though the student knows the instructor is near. However, anxiety will reduce once the student begins to experience success in their training—which develops confidence—and they become familiar with the new environment.

Ironically, anxiety returns each time the environment changes or the level of risk increases. Instructors expect anxiety levels to increase as the student moves from the shallow to deep water in the swimming pool, and again when the student moves to the open ocean. In each case, additional exposures to an environment combined with positive experiences, increase confidence and reduce stress.

Understanding the bond between confidence, experience and stress levels is an important concept for survival instructors. The selection of techniques, training schedules and training exercises can make a substantial difference in how students perceive a stimulus after leaving the classroom.

Finally, students must be trained to recognize the symptoms leading to hypervigilance and to apply stress management techniques that will quickly reduce the heart rate. This chapter will examine two techniques, breathing and visualization. Breathing drills force the heart rate to slowdown, while visualization techniques mentally prepare the student for the unknown. Both techniques can affect immediate changes in anxiety levels and the heart rate.

SURVIVAL STRESS MANAGEMENT

TRAINING GOALS

DEVELOPING:

SKILL CONFIDENCE

EXPERIENCE

THROUGH DYNAMIC TRAINING EXERCISES

VISUALIZATION

➤ PREDICT POTENTIAL THREAT CUES
➤ PROGRAM PROPER RESPONSE
➤ PROGRAM PLAN B

BREATH CONTROL

Following is a quick check list which highlights design methodologies to reduce survival stress. The methodology should evolve around four goals:

1. To increase a student's confidence in a skill at a subconscious level quickly.
2. To increase a student's situational confidence through stimulus response training exercises.
3. To use visualization principles to mentally prepare the student for the potential threat stimulus and the correct response.
4. To train students how to use breath control to slow down the heart rate when anxiety arises.

Confidence

Consider the mental and physical affects of confidence. How often have you heard about an individual's poor performance being attributed to the lack of confidence? In contrast, have you ever heard of an athlete's exceptional performance described as relaxed and full of confidence?

Confidence implies a mental state which is void of fear, anxiety or self doubt. The mind and the body may be alerted to the needs of the present task, but the mental state is relaxed with the knowledge of individual competence. When a person is confident in their ability, they are relaxed but alert, their ability to concentrate is focused, and their heart rate and breath control are steady.

The lack of confidence implies a mental state that produces anxiety and stress. Pargman (1986) states, "Stress is an unsettling reactive experience to external factors. Your reactions to environmental stimuli may be positive or negative, supportive or destructive. If you perceive them as being negative, then the stimuli are negative."

The effects of negative stress have been documented throughout the last three chapters. At a very low level, negative stress affects a student's concentration. In *The Mental Athlete*, Porter and Foster (1986) report "When an athlete chokes, it is usually because he or she is fearful or angry. A tennis player for example may begin choking and missing every shot, and becoming more upset with himself/ herself. The player has lost the 'present' focus—that of staying in the present moment—and continues to think of the blown shots and mistakes made in the past. Combined with negative thinking, this process interferes with concentration, focus and confidence."

The affects of confidence have a very profound outcome on survival performance. As a state of mind, we know that a confident mindset maintains lower heart rates which are critical to cognitive processing and survival skill performance. Therefore, the training process must be designed to enhance confidence at a subconscious level.

The development of subconscious confidence begins with helping a student become secure with a specific technique. In chapter one, we examined the psychology associated with technique simplicity. The student's perception of the speed at which a technique can be learned is directly related to the student's motivation levels. A student who perceives a survival skill is not attainable quickly, will not be motivated to practice, resulting in a lower level of skill confidence and competence.

Chapter three took this concept to another level. The relationship between stress, heart rate and performance, provides trainers with a very important foundation for designing survival systems. The research findings stipulate that only gross motor skills will be able to withstand the affects of survival stress. And since it is reasonable to believe a student's heart rate will exceed 145 BPM when exposed to a life threatening stimulus, the training of fine and complex motor skills should be avoided whenever possible. Therefore, technique simplicity must be examined from the perspectives of student perception, the speed a student may learn a skill, and the effects the heart rate has on skill execution.

Dynamic Training Exercises

As a psychological state, anxiety is common when a student perceives lack of control or lack of confidence. Anxiety continues to increase when the situational demands escalate and the time needed to manage the situation decreases. Therefore, training exercises must be developed to decrease anxiety for predictable field events and increase situational confidence.

Developing situational confidence is a matter of applying a technique to the dynamics of a field application. This process uses stimulus response training principles and allows the student to explore how a technique will function outside the static atmosphere of the classroom. When stimulus response training principles are designed and monitored correctly, the student's reaction and response times are dramatically reduced.

Reducing reaction and response time is one of the most important functions of survival training. Unfortunately, many instructors never move beyond simple static practice. Although static practice allows students to develop basic neural motor programs, static practice will not trigger the motor program when exposed to a spontaneous threat.

An example of static training is the typical law enforcement firearms qualification course. The typical course uses a procedure where the student practices statically by shooting paper targets for a score. The targets will normally consist of a human silhouette, accompanied with a scoring system based upon target location. Officers are graded based upon their proficiency by shooting tight groups in the vital organ portions of the target.

From a learning perspective, this type of firearms course will only measure fundamental marksmanship proficiency. However, this course will not measure an officer's ability to perceive a deadly force stimulus and return fire under the dynamic conditions of an actual fire fight. In fact, fundamental firearms marksmanship training will do nothing to trigger a survival response.

Enhancing reaction and response time is a matter of developing triggering mechanisms into the training process. This can be accomplished in the same manner as the average driver education course. The typical drivers education course begins by putting students in a driving simulator, which trains the students in the fundamental skills. The second stage consists of putting the student in a vehicle on an empty parking lot, where the basic motor programs are applied in a controlled field environment. Once the fundamental skills have been refined in the controlled environment, the student progresses to driving in the dynamic environment of street traffic. It is during this final phase that the student begins to interact with environmental stimuli. Skills such as emergency steering and braking are refined, and with minimal practice become automatic.

Consider how fast a new driver learns and reacts to a red light, a pedestrian jay walking, or another vehicle running a red light. In each case, new drivers learn to react appropriately after one or two near misses. Very quickly, new drivers learn to react to emergencies automatically, with little thought.

In many ways, firearms training is comparable to drivers education. Both skills are conducted in dynamic, constantly changing environments. Both skills are based upon complex skill execution which requires timing, accuracy and reactive capabilities. And both skills can be classified as open/reactionary motor skills with life defending capabilities.

True combat firearms training is based upon teaching students to fire at a human opponent who is exhibiting a life threatening stimulus. Without this type of stimulus, trainers cannot expect their students to respond automatically and accurately in their first combat experience.

The most advanced methods of combat firearms training is through the use of dynamic training exercises. These exercises use modified weapon systems which can fire plastic bullets, cotton wads or dye marking devices. Dynamic training provides a relatively safe training environment where the officer engages a live human in a simulated deadly force encounter.

Although the use of red handle exercises has only recently become popular, red handle firearms training can be dated back to the early 1900s to W.E. Fairbairn. As a member of the Shang Hai Police Department, Fairbairn was requested to identify training methods which would enhance an officer's reaction time and survivability.

At the time, the police department's firearms course centered around a qualification course shooting a bull's-eye target. Fairbairn concluded the qualification based upon shooting a bull's-eye target, was not preparing officers for the dynamics of a fire fight. Quite brilliantly, Fairbairn developed the first recorded police combat shooting course in 1921. The course consisted of officers searching a warehouse and engaging subjects using plastic bullets. (Robert Welsch, of the Ohio State Patrol, advanced dynamic training methods in the middle 1970s with the development of cotton wad projectiles. Today, the most popular method of red handle training is with dye marking bullets or paint balls.)

The primary advantage of dynamic training exercises is the experience of interacting with an open environment. Each exposure to a threat stimulus allows the student a chance to identify the subtle cues, which can only be gained through experience. Each exposure allows students an opportunity to work out solutions and program the correct survival response. Janis, DeFares and Grossman (1983) state, "stress inoculation procedures generally include the same basic components, informative warnings about what to expect, which make people aware of their vulnerability to realistic sources of threat; reassuring information about positive features of the situation and social coping resources that build up self-confidence about being able to tolerate and master the ordeal."

Even though there are many advantages to dynamic training exercises, it is important to structure the exercise to maximize the learning and develop confidence. Too many times, instructors create a role playing where the student has no chance of winning. If the student is exposed to only one no-win scenario, the student does not have the chance to identify the threat cues, select the appropriate survival response and develop confidence in their ability to manage the threat. No win scenarios are destructive and should be avoided if positive feedback cannot be supplied.

The following are a few considerations which should be observed when designing dynamic training exercises.

1.   The exercise should have clear goals and objectives which relate to a dynamic field encounter.
2.   The role players should be dedicated to making the exercise a learning experience, not a match of physical prowess or a battle of the egos.
3.   After the first exercise, the student should receive clear feedback on the threat cues which he missed and the proper response selection.
4.   Second, third and fourth exercises should immediately follow so the student can identify the threat cues.

Visualization

Visualization techniques are not new to the training field. Olympic athletes have been using visualization since the early 1970s religiously. The studies substantiating the positive attributes of visualization are still debated. However, there are several theories worth noting.

The Psychoneuromuscular Theory suggests that mental practice innervates the muscles used during a skill. Schmidt (1987) proposes that mental practice initiates low level innervation in the muscles and the Golgi tendons. The feedback from the Golgi tendons is relayed to the premotor cortex and strengthens the motor program.

This theory provides a basis for spinal tuning, a term describing the process of preparing the motor nervous system for a specific action. Spinal tuning is the process of identifying the correct survival motor program and pre-activating the nervous system before the motor program is needed. In essence, the nervous system is warmed up and in a hold pattern waiting for the activation command.

The Symbolic Learning Theory (Denis, 1985) examines the psychological benefits of visualization. The theory hypothesizes "that mental practice benefits performance because it allows the participant to cognitively prepare for and plan performance. The sequential aspects of the task can be rehearsed, task goals can be clarified, potential problems in performance can be identified, and effective procedures for task execution can be planned" (Murphy & Jowdy, 1992).

The Symbolic Learning Theory focuses on the pre-planning component of performance. Anxiety and the escalating heart rates occur when a student is exposed to a potential threat and is unclear on the outcome. Preparation in any form provides a student with an opportunity to think through potential threats and the proper survival response before being exposed to the threat.

Survival visualization and mental preparation should be taught as a method of reducing survival stress and reestablishing confidence. Survival visualization should be segmented into the following three components:

Predict the potential threat cues: As an example, consider the danger of a police officer making a traffic stop. Officers routinely face deadly force threats when they approach a stopped vehicle for a traffic misdemeanor. One of the most dangerous points of a traffic stop is when the officer is halfway between the subject's vehicle and patrol car. A trained officer should consider that an armed subject intending to shoot the officer will have to exit the vehicle to gain clear acquisition. Important threat cues to warn the officer would include the subject watching the officer intently through the rear view mirror, looking for witnesses and exiting the vehicle without his right hand grabbing the steering wheel, dash board or door jamb. (The latter is based upon the fact that the majority of individuals are right handed.) Any of these cues should alert the officer there is an imminent deadly force threat.

Pre-program the proper survival response: Once the predictable threat cues are visited, the student should then visualize himself responding with the correct survival response. In reference to the police officer making a traffic stop, the correct response would be to move laterally to cover while retrieving his weapon. Once the officer can secure cover, he should visualize how he will gain proper target aquisition.

Pre-program a plan B (Failure Factor): Developing alternate plans assures the officer that if the primary plan fails, he has a backup which has been thought through. Backup plans are very important in establishing personal skill confidence and maintaining control over survival stress.

Students of visualization believe this process will pre-program the nervous system and reduce reaction time, while preparing the student mentally for a deadly encounter. Visualization not only warms up the nervous system, but also reduces cognitive anxiety leading to hypervigilance.

Breath Control
The relationship between breath control and the ability to concentrate or focus has been recognized for centuries. Ancient philosophy and martial art texts abound with references drawing parallels between combat performance, breath control and the ability to focus and concentrate when exposed to survival stress. Today, scientists are beginning to unveil many of the secrets of breath control and believe hypervigilance is linked to hyperventilation.

Hyperventilation (rapid breathing) is a stress response which induces immediate changes in the body. Symptoms associated with hyperventilation are impairments in memory, concentration and diminished discriminative or perceptual abilities. All of these functions are critical to survival awareness and reaction time.

Recent research indicates that hyperventilation causes "the reduction of CO_2 in the bloodstream and a concomitant lowering of blood acid level, numerous systemic alterations are like to occur in the body. These include increased sympathetic activity, changes in renal function, increased risk of cardiac dysrhythmias, elevation of the heart rate, decreased oxygen supply to brain tissue, and heightened cerebral vasoconstriction. . . Numerous studies clearly indicate that voluntary changes in breathing pattern can modify one's ability to cope with pain and with threatening fear-provoking situations. Some of these investigations have shown that slowing down the respiratory frequency increases depth of breathing significantly, reduces the subjective experience of anxiety under stressful conditions, and raises one's threshold of tolerance to pain. Voluntarily increasing respiratory frequency, on the other hand, seems to have the opposite effects. Additional reports indicated that voluntary changes of the breathing pattern can enhance certain mental abilities involved in the acquisition and processing of new information" (Janis, DeFares & Grossman, 1983).

There are many different methods of controlled breathing, but two key components are present in all systems; slow deep breaths expanding the belly and controlling the respiration cycle. Expanding the lung capacity is a process called "belly breathing." The technique involves inhaling and allowing the stomach to expand. Unlike shallow rapid breaths, this procedure forces the lungs to expand to their fullest capacity, bringing in more oxygen for the system. This procedure also expands the length of the inhale and also helps to slow down the respiration rate.

The second component is the respiration cycle. The technique advocates inhaling for a specified count (normally three seconds), holding the breath for three seconds and controlling the exhale for three seconds. After repeating the technique for three cycles, students will find their heart rate will lower, perceptual and cognitive tasks become more acute, and motor performance will increase.

How important is breath control? We could argue that breath control should be a mandatory component of survival stress management. Once students have learned the symptoms associated with survival stress, (awareness of increased heart rate, rapid breathing, abnormal sweating, and uncontrollable muscle tremors), students will know they are outside of their survival performance zone and initiate controlled breathing exercises.

Chapter Five Summary

A consistent theme in this text is the role the heart rate has on combat performance. The research clearly demonstrates catastrophic failures in cognitive processing (perception, identification, response selection) and motor performance when the heart rate accelerates.

This chapter explored this issue further. The research suggests that anxiety and/or stress are by-products of a perception of a threat and may lead to hypervigilance if the student believes the threat is lethal, imminent, and the ability to control the threat is insufficient. However, stress is a matter of perception, and perceptions can be changed through the training process.

The beginning of this text proposed a simple theory: all aspects of survival and combat training should be designed to develop a student's confidence. This theory establishes design guidelines focusing on technique simplicity, linking the number of response options and the development of training exercises designed to give students realistic experiences. A design methodology based upon these basic premises enhances confidence, reduces the heart rate during combat, and minimizes the potential of hypervigilance from occurring.

Chapter Five References

Alexander, J., Groller, R. and Morris, J. (1990) *The Warrior's Edge*, Morrow Publishing.

Benson, H. (1975) *The Relaxation Response*, Avon Books

Denis, M. (1985) *Visual Imagery and the Use of Mental Practice in the Development of Motor Skills.* Unpublished Doctoral Dissertation.

Janis, I.L. and Mann, L. (1977) *Decision Making: A Psychological Analysis of Conflict, Choice and Commitment.*

Janis, I.L., Defares, P. and Grossman, P. (1983) *Selye's Guide to Stress Research, Van* Nostrauz Reinholz Publishing.

McGrath, J.E. (1970) *Social and Psychological Factors in Stress*, Holt, Rinehart and Winston

Murphy, S. and Jowdy, D. (1992) *Advances in Sports Psychology*, (Chapter 11), Human Kinetics Publishing.

Pargman, (1986) *Stress and Motor Performance: Understanding and Coping.* Mouvment Publications.

Porter, K. and Foster, J. (1986) *The Mental Athlete*, William C. Brown Publishers.

Schmidt, R. (1987) *Motor Control and Learning,* 2nd Edition, Human Kinetics.

Whitesell, P., (1989) *The Psychology of Intimidation and the Physical Conflict in the Police Profession,* PPCT Research Publications.

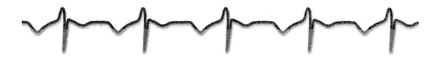

6

Implementing Survival Research

"One of the biggest reasons for failure in the field of battle is not what to do next . . . this is the result of not having been trained thoroughly in what to expect on the battlefield."

General Orlando Ward, 1954

The body of research reviewed in the first five chapters established a foundation for designing a survival or combat training system. The focus of the research has been to examine several critical aspects of survival performance. Most importantly, the research stipulates that exposure to a perceived threat stimulus automatically activates the sympathetic nervous system, which in turn accelerates the heart. Under these conditions, cognitive processing deteriorates, leading to perceptual narrowing and hypervigilance.

The research has also examined design principles centering around simplicity. We found that simple gross motor skills, when combined with minimal response options, have a better chance of withstanding the affects of survival stress. Now it is time to bring the research together and provide a model for designing a survival system.

To maintain a consistency in the training methodology, remember that all survival training should evolve around three basic goals. They include: 1) identifying techniques which are compatible to the affects of stress, 2) developing training exercises which will enhance survival reaction time (neural programming), and 3) adopting training methods that enhance a student's confidence, thus reducing anxiety and lowering the heart rate.

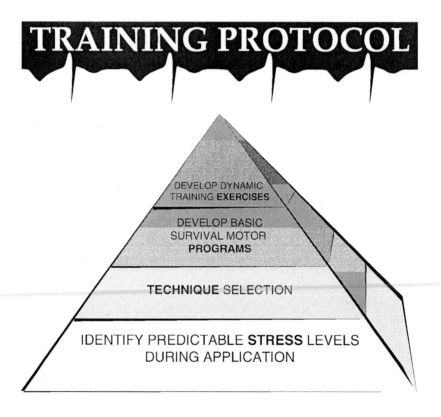

TRAINING PROTOCOL

DEVELOP DYNAMIC
TRAINING **EXERCISES**

DEVELOP BASIC
SURVIVAL MOTOR
PROGRAMS

TECHNIQUE SELECTION

IDENTIFY PREDICTABLE **STRESS** LEVELS
DURING APPLICATION

The design process focuses on four simple steps. They include:

- Identifying predictable stress levels during application
- Technique selection
- Developing basic survival motor programs
- Developing dynamic training exercises

To demonstrate this process, the author has selected combat handgun firearms training as the model. Firearms training is a common and necessary skill in the criminal justice and military roles. Besides being a high liability skill with criminal and civil implications of negligence, firearms procedures and stances are still hotly debated.

More importantly, the tactical application of a firearm in combat combines a complex skill execution under the most extreme pressures of survival stress. Along with the criminal and civil ramification of required accuracy, the student's survival will depend upon the instructor's skill in the system design.

Identifying Predictable Stress Levels During Application

The first step of designing any survival or combat system is attempting to identify the level of stress in which performance will occur. Identifying stress levels provides a parameter of heart rate activity, which also identifies motor skill capabilities (gross, fine or complex). This step allows instructors to select the most appropriate skill classifications based upon the Inverted-U Hypothesis.

Combat firearms skills could be considered one of the most stressful encounters any student will face. With the exception of sniper tactics, combat firearms skills will be used in life threatening environments. Therefore, we can assume that heart rate activity will exceed 175 or 200 BPM. At this level of stress, we know that fine and complex motor skills should be avoided and the number of response options should be kept to a minimum.

Technique Selection

Selecting skills should be a simple procedure based upon the Inverted-U research. This process provides instructors with a scale which matches optimal skill performance to specified heart rate zones. As an example, the research clearly indicates that fine or complex motor skills are not compatible to high stress environments. In contrast, gross motor skills appear to be more natural or instinctive, and are more conducive to high stress environments.

From this research, one hypothesis that can be developed is that complex shooting stances and procedures will result in poor accuracy. In *Biological Limits of Police Combat Handgun Shooting Accuracy* (1994), Vila and Morrison examined related research which questions the performance limitations of combat handgun skills. They state that over the last 100 years, police officer accuracy has been consistently poor. Furthermore, they propose that "the body's nervous and mechanical systems place a finite limit on combat handgun shooting accuracy. . . Our results support the hypothesis and indicate that physical limits to police combat handgun shooting accuracy must be better understood before valid training can be developed."

Vila and Morrison's study, combined with the re-searched cited throughout this text, establishes the dominant control the sympathetic nervous system has over survival performance. This is especially true in combat (hand-gun) firearms skills.

Historically, combat firearms training was heavily influenced by the research of W. E. Fairbairn. In the pursuit of enhancing the survival of Shang Hai police officers, Fairbairn accompanied men into combat and observed how they responded naturally when confronting armed assailants. His research resulted in the development of the early forms of the one hand point shooting stances and the two-handed Isosceles. The single-hand point shooting stance was developed for close range assailants, while the two-handed Isosceles was for greater distance and more precise shooting.

After Fairbairn left the Shang Hai police, he moved to England and began teaching for the Department of Ministry. Through joint U. S. and Britain training exercises, he met Col. Rex Applegate (U.S. Army, now retired). Applegate continued the research into these two stances and developed them to a more precise shooting system. However, Applegate never lost sight of the goal of keeping the skills simple and naturally reflexive (instinctive).

Since the early 1980's the Weaver Stance became the popular and dominant combat stance in many law enforcement circles. This side-canted stance is reported to be bio-mechanically stronger, and conducive to defensive tactics training. In theory, these arguments make sense. Weaver does provide a more stable platform, but believing the arm and grip positions provide a stronger grip is incorrect compared to kinesiology principles relating to the natural arc of strength. Burroughs (1993) states, "officers in the field can only respond to situations requiring the use of force with the skills they possess. More importantly, they can only respond with gross motor skills that have less likelihood for failure during conditions of stress."

In *Selection of Upper Torso Shooting Stances Utilizing Kinesiology Principles* (1995), Tanji states, "The natural arc of strength can be described as the natural swinging motion of the arms to the front while in a standing position. The physiological explanation can be described as a natural muscle positioning of the arms which will provide maximum contraction of specific muscles . . . to achieve maximum muscular hand strength anywhere in this arc . . . The Isosceles stance arm position falls closer within the natural arc of strength than the Weaver stance. While in the Modified Isosceles stance, the upper body and extremity muscles are in their relative anatomical position to exert maximum contraction."

Another debate evolves around the use of the front sight. Students of Applegate suggest that in the stress of combat, they will not take the time to align the sights before shooting. Instead, they will look through the sights. Proponents of precision shooting state that men can use the sights in combat if they are trained correctly. Furthermore, the threat of litigation and the high liability associated with any law enforcement shooting necessitates the use of the front sight.

There is no doubt the liability concerns are valid. However, *the sympathetic nervous system will control and dominate all motor action when a student is confronted with a spontaneous deadly force threat.* Vila and Morrison's observation is correct; the firearms community has been remiss in researching physiological responses to survival stress and designing training around these reactions.

When designing any high stress survival skill, instructors must accept the dominance the sympathetic nervous system has on motor performance. For example, the biological model of shooting a hand weapon deals with the sympathetic nervous system and the visual response to a threat. The activation of sympathetic system causes a greater release of the neurotransmitters, initiating the sympathetic alarm response. Large portions of the sympathetic system often become stimulated simultaneously, a phenomenon called mass discharge, which is automatic and virtually uncontrollable.

Humans are binocular, or two-eyed creatures. Both eyes are needed to process information from the environment. This occurs as a survival requirement of the body to receive more light and information to process the situation and formulate a response. The body will not allow one eye to close, partially due to the sympathetic response, partly due to the body's need to survive. When one eye is closed or concealed, more that 60% of the needed sensory information is not relayed to the part of the brain that process the input and directs the output (Breedlove & Siddle, 1995).

Under stress, the sympathetic nervous system will adjust the body to receive as much information as possible to survive the threat. The body and visual system will automatically move to a position, allowing the visual system maximum information to deal with the threat. Automatic survival responses dictating the need for binocular vision occur when the officer is exposed to spontaneous, life threatening stimulus and the time to respond is very short.

The contemporary Weaver Stance is based upon a side-cant of the body and head. The canting of the body indirectly pulls the head sideways so the officer must establish sight alignment with his dominant eye. This stance is theoretically sound and biomechanically supported. However, single eye acquisition slows the visual processing time, resulting in a slower response time.

Historically, research by W.E. Fairbairn and Rex Applegate demonstrated that men in combat will square on the target. The development of the Isosceles Stance, body squared on the target with both arms extended towards the target, was designed by observing the natural actions of men in combat. Applegate (1994) reports the stance "is instinctively resorted to by the officer when the target is shooting back." Applegate's association of firearms and survival stress is on point. He identifies the Isosceles Stance as the natural and instinctive stance for situations where survival stress is peaked.

In situations where time is short, the brain will demand more information and pull the head square to obtain binocular vision. This gives the brain more information for target selection and reduces response time. One reason this occurs is that the eyes cannot focus during survival stress.

Focusing of the lens is a function of the parasympathetic nervous system, which is responsible for activities associated with bodily conservation and maintaining of resources. The lens is normally held in a flattened, distance viewing state by tension of the radial ligaments. Parasympathetic excitement contracts the ciliary muscle, which releases this tension, allowing the lens to become more convex. This causes the eye to focus on close objects. During sympathetic response, the eye cannot focus; thus one will see the front sight out of focus which will result in a heightened state of stress.

The primary advantage of the Isosceles Stance is the ability to use both eyes naturally. "Both eyes have to be open for engagement when tracking a moving target. This does not matter if the assailant or the officer is moving. As binocular or two-eyed individuals, many of the body's functions are dependent on the efficiency of both eyes being open and working together. These functions include balance, depth perception, bodily movement, tracking and eye-hand-body coordination" (Breedlove, 1995).

There are many reasons that two-eyed shooting is superior to monocular or one-eyed shooting. However, the activation of the sympathetic nervous system changes the function of the eye, inhibiting the ability to focus on the front sight. When a person is required to look at a near object (front sight), the pupils must constrict. This is an involuntary response to enhance the "depth of focus." During sympathetic activation, the pupils dilate or enlarge to allow the body to receive more light and information. Therefore, trying to use the front sights during survival stress is counterproductive to the natural function of the eye. Binocular shooting allows the eye to function normally. Additional advantages of binocular shooting are:

- Visual sensitivity, or the ability to respond to movements is twice as great.
- Less light is needed.
- For a visual cortex cell in the brain to fire efficiently, there needs to be summation of signal to the eyes.
- Monocular deprivation causes disruption of cortical connections.
- The following of a moving target is binocularly monitored.
- With binocular, there is a 20-30% improvement in visual motor tasks, (trained responses) over monocular.
- Distances less that 20 feet need binocular vision for maximum visual input.

The basis of tracking has to be precluded by the biological facts of the optic nerve. Common thought is that the eyes "see" and nothing else. That statement could not be further from the truth. The optic nerve as it comes out behind the eye meets with the nerve of the other eye and splits in two, transversing around the brain in its path to the occipital cortex on the back of the brain. Along the way, this nerve branches off at different intervals to innervate all parts of the functioning brain. Less than 70% of the original nerve actually reaches the occipital cortex.

Part of the nerve goes to the balance centers of the body, the vestibular cortex. Balance is binocularly monitored. You can try this yourself by patching one eye and trying to go about your daily routine. You will not want to continue very long. The eyes tell the body where it is in space. This is very difficult with one eye closed. The body will reject the situation and leave you with a feeling of low confidence. To be in balance, the body must receive stimulus from both eyes equally; thus the body will move into a position to maximize binocular vision.

Depth perception, the ability of knowing the location in space of an object or threat, is critical for distances less than 20 feet where most officer confrontations occur. The body will receive incorrect distance determinations and poor judgmental decisions will be made under monocular conditions.

The results of this research eliminate the "instinctive" aspects of Isosceles styles of shooting. Instead, the research illustrates the Isosceles stance and single-hand point instinct stance are based upon natural and predictable responses resulting from the activation of the sympathetic nervous system. The author hypothesizes the Isosceles stance is not a shooting stance, but a stress response platform—based upon the dominant need for visual information and the natural arc of strength, which places the body in the most natural position for maximum survival stress performance.

Furthermore, the research generates a need to divide firearms training into spontaneous and nonspontaneous combat skills. For example, stress and the sympathetic nervous system are initiated when time to respond is minimal and the distance to the target is relatively short. Stances best suited for close range acquisition are;

Single-hand point shooting within two to three yards: There is a valid argument stating that at any range students should assume a two-handed grip. The proponents of this philosophy believe that the weapon is better controlled and stabilized, resulting in better accuracy. However, when students are within close proximity of a target and time to respond is perceived as very minimal (half second or less), students will automatically resort to a single-hand stance, even if they are only trained in two-handed stances. The key to stress response is the perception of time and distance. Somehow, the brain recognizes that the time required to acquire the target with two hands takes longer than with one hand - and will override all previous training to engage the threat more quickly. However, this automatic override seems to disengage as the distances increase and the need for accuracy gets greater.

Modified Isosceles two-handed stance for three yards or more: At distances beginning at two or three yards, the brain will recognize the increased need for accuracy and will automatically respond by assuming a two-handed grip with the weapon raising to eye level. Additionally, the activation of the sympathetic nervous system will cause the head and shoulders to square on the target to obtain maximum visual input, with the arms assuming some variation of an upper body Isosceles.

From a training perspective, the author would recommend the dominant placement foot to the rear. This stance will increase platform stability. "Body balance, mobility and overall body symmetry is enhanced by dropping the dominant foot to the rear a distance of one half its length, beginning square to the target, while maintaining shoulder width separation" (Burroughs, 1995). However, whether the student will actually assume this stance in combat is unknown.

The important points of the Modified Isosceles are not the fine points of a stance. The key points are squaring the head on the target and bringing the weapon to eye level so the student can see through the sights with both eyes open.

Modified Weaver for nonspontaneous activities: Westmoreland's observations of red handle exercises show when officers have time, distance and cover, or when time allows absolute precision, the officer may utilize some form of the Weaver Stance. These situations would include barricade shooting or moving while covering a target or firezone. However, the stress of the situation is not as high and the sympathetic nervous system is not activated to maximum levels. Under these conditions, the sympathetic nervous system is not activated and using the dominant eye for sight alignment is preferable and possible.

What Fairbairn started in the 1920's and Applegate advanced is a combat firearms system based upon the observation of natural responses while in the stress of combat. In contrast, Weaver was born in the closed non-stress environment of competition. Yet, proponents of Weaver have criticized Applegate for sticking to a shooting system which is not "biomechanically stronger and assures better accuracy."

Based upon sympathetic nervous system activation, visual dominance, the natural arc of strength, and motor skill capabilities under stress, it is apparent that Applegate was correct in the design of his combat firearms system. Applegate's logic based upon observations of combat responses and his intuitive beliefs can now be proven scientifically. However, designing any survival system is not about proving one style correct and another wrong. Designing survival and combat training is about preparing men and women for combat, in any method which will assure their survival. Fairbairn and Applegate did not have the research which is available today about performance and stress. However, they did conduct empirical research by observation, which in many ways is more important than clinically validated research.

Developing Basic Survival Motor Programs

Once the techniques of the combat firearms training have been identified, the next step is to begin the training process. This process begins by creating a need for the specific skills to be taught. This classroom unit would address:

- An explanation of common situations requiring the need for combat firearms training (traffic stops, felony stops, tactical entries, building searches). This unit would examine specific aspects of assaults, including distances to the target, the profile of the assailant and other variables designed to motivate the student to train.

- An explanation of the firearms skills they will learn. The explanation should include why the techniques were selected (based upon stress responses, the distances to the target, etc.) and the techniques that should be performed in combat.

The second stage is the process of beginning to establish the basic neural muscular motor program. Remember, this unit should be designed to help the students believe they can learn the skill quickly and to establish confidence quickly. Since learning a survival motor skill is based upon modeling the instructor, all technique demonstrations should be designed to present clear pictures to Short Term Sensory Store (the mind's eye), so the students can replicate the demonstration. Therefore, the instructor should follow the training rules established in Chapter one.

- All demonstrations should never exceed 50% speed or power. This will enable the students to "see" the components of the technique more quickly.
- All skills should be taught in three components, the beginning, middle and end. This simplifies learning any motor skill and allows the students the ability to understand the academics of technique execution.
- All verbal and demonstration feedback should be designed to create mental pictures of the correct technique application. It is important for instructors to remember that the picture in the mind's eye is the model from which all neural motor programs are developed.

The third stage of developing the basic survival motor program is creating a positive training experience. The range activities should be structured so the students establish shooting confidence very soon in the training process. As an example, consider beginning all firearms training at close ranges using slow speeds. This provides the students with positive accuracy and gives time to sort out the academics of the technique. Remember, technique cannot be corrected unless the students understand what they are doing wrong. Speed should only be increased after the class (as a unit,) is exhibiting positive performance.

Developing Dynamic Training Exercises

As identified in the last chapter, the purpose of dynamic training exercises is to provide the students with the tactical or combat environment in which the combat skills will be executed. The benefits of dynamic training exercises include:

- The reduction in survival reaction time by providing a learning experience, where the threat and outcome are processed analytically. This learning experience allows the students to access threats and the combat response more quickly in the dynamics of a real encounter.
- The training exercise gives the students a safe environment to work out the tactical aspects of a survival skill.
- If the training exercise is designed correctly, the students will have a positive experience with the survival skill. The effectiveness of the skill will

increase personal confidence in managing a similar situation, resulting in lower heart rates during a field encounter.

The development of dynamic training exercises should follow the same process as teaching an individual skill. Once the purpose of the training exercise has been identified (creating the need), the instructor should break down the lesson of the dynamic training exercise into three components.

Attempting to illustrate all of the combat firearms scenarios which criminal justice officers and military soldiers may encounter would require a separate text. For example, criminal justice officers would need to design exercises for traffic stops, felony stops, building searches, hostage rescue and tactical entries. The list for military personnel would be even longer. Therefore, the author has selected tactical entry leading to a building search as a design model. This mission is common to both criminal justice and military operations. It also involves using a handgun in a moving dynamic environment where the students will experience intermittent high levels of stress.

Phase One: The first phase begins by introducing the fundamentals of tactical room entries. In this phase the students will be given a broad overview of the components of entering a room, clearing the nearest corner and moving to a position of control. This phase should encourage questions about the techniques of each movement, so the students can process and comprehend their responsibility before they enter the training exercise. Taking this time is important, for analytical understanding must be accomplished before physical competence can be expected.

Once the fundamentals of the entry and search are examined, the tactical aspects of survival stress should be addressed. This block of instruction examines where predictable points of survival stress will surface and how to control the stress through breathing and visualization. For example, a team's first exposure to survival stress will occur just before the entry. Most officers or soldiers can expect to feel some form of survival stress, such as increased heart rates, hyperventilation, cotton mouth, sweaty palms and muscle tremors due to an increase in adrenal activity. These stress manifestations are normal and are not necessarily a sign of fear. However, once these stress symptoms surface, the students must immediately recognize they are outside of their combat performance heart range.

Diffusing the effects of survival stress is a matter of training students to include visualization and breathing drills as a component of the survival response. For example, before initiating each high risk activity, students should conduct a quick mental check list. The list should include where threats may develop, what is the primary response option and what is the secondary response option. Once the students have visualized and spinal tuned the nervous system, they should begin the breathing drills to assist in reducing the heart rate. This procedure should be repeated before each high risk encounter.

The application of these drills to a tactical entry and building search is a matter of identifying predictable stress points. The most obvious stress point is before the initial entry, followed by the entry into subsequent uncleared rooms. Therefore, the instructor should help the students visualize how they will deploy, where the expected threats may develop, what skills are needed to neutralize the threat, followed by the breathing drills.

Realistically, instructors can't expect students to remember the stress management techniques when they first practice. However, instructors must reinforce the relationship between stress management techniques and combat performance.

Phase Two: Phase two involves a slow motion walk-through of the fundamental steps of clearing the room. This phase begins with a brief review of the entry procedures by allowing the students to see a demonstration at slow speed. During this demonstration, the instructor should reinforce instructional points reviewed in the classroom with a physical demonstration. This helps the students visualize and ultimately begins the soft wiring process of neural motor program development.

Phase Three: This phase allows the students to practice the fundamentals of room clearing. The instructor would segment tactical entries into three general components; moving through the doorway quickly, clearing the immediate corner and moving to a position of control. It is important that each component of the entry is clearly instructed to ensure quick learning.

Each step of clearing the room should be taught in sequence and practiced individually until the students have the mechanics generally correct. Only then should the next step in the sequence be practiced. After all of the sequences have been practiced individually, then the students are ready to practice the whole movement.

Phase Four: Now that the students have learned the fundamentals of tactical room clearing, the students are ready to combine the firearms range exercises to the dynamics of entering a room under fire. This phase would begin using simulated ammunition (cotton wads or dye marking ammunition) on a static target, placed in the first corner of entry.

Students would begin the exercise with the survival stress management techniques, followed by walking into the room and engaging the target while moving. It is important to start this process slowly, which provides the students the chance to work out the mechanics of moving and shooting together. As the competence level increases, the pace of the entry should be increased until moving at full speed and consistently hitting the target accurately. Once this phase has been completed, the instructor should begin moving the static target to different locations. Generally, within three entries the students will be accurately hitting the target.

The final step of phase four would include the use of multiple shoot/don't shoot targets. This step begins the process of teaching target discrimination.

Phase Five: Phase five advances the students to engage another human being with the simulated ammunition. The human target should be equipped with safety protection equipment and only exhibit threatening actions. An example would be raising a firearm towards the student upon entry.

Once the students know they will be facing a live aggressor, instructors will visibly notice an increase in student's stress levels. Again, the stress management techniques must be reinforced to assist students in lowering their heart rates.

The students should begin the drills with slow entries and engage the target upon threat identification. Do not be surprised to find accuracy poor in the first couple of repetitions. Remember that the threat stimulus just changed from a static target to a live human being. However, somewhere between three and five repetitions the accuracy will increase. As the level of accuracy increases, the speed of the entry should increase accordingly.

Phase Six: This phase begins the process of allowing the target to fire back with the simulated ammunition. Again, expect the accuracy levels to drop in the beginning. This is because the stimulus changes, which increases the threat level and the associated stress/heart rate.

During this phase, the instructor should restrict the threat to a single target. Restrict the assailant role player to keep the threat simple and quick. This helps the students to enhance visual reaction time and begin training the eye to identify a threat more quickly.

Phase Seven: The final phase consists of several scenarios which test the student's reactions and accuracy to the fullest. The scenarios should be realistic, but designed to instruct target discrimination. Do not allow the assailants to "screw" with the students. The student goals for these training exercises are threat recognition, quicker reaction time, and increased confidence in their ability to manage a life-threatening assailant.

Finally, instructors should reinforce the survival stress management techniques as often as possible. These skills are easily overlooked as dynamic training develops. However, combat firearms accuracy is directly related to the ability to control stress and heart rates. Students must learn that survival stress management is just as important as practicing any survival skill.

Instructors should also recognize that students will need two to three exposures to a threat stimulus before their survival responses become automatic and fluid. Expect the students to freeze, implement the wrong response or hesitate the first couple of repetitions. Use these failures as learning examples and articulate to students the pitfalls associated with failures. Immediately provide positive feed- back and walk students through the correct response.

One final point worth mentioning. Scenario development should ultimately test discretion. A final series of scenarios should provide shoot/don't shoot situations to ensure that students do not become indirectly conditioned to shoot in every confrontation.

Chapter Six Summary

Designing survival and combat training has inherent instructor liabilities. The days are gone where instructors can blame poor student performance on lack of motivation or the student's physical competence. The author admits that instructors will encounter difficult learners, but the average student can respond quickly to training if the training is researched and delivered in a logical method.

The disparity in student performance between the classroom and the field is often the result of teaching skills which are not compatible for high stress environments, or because the instructor never linked the skill to a threat stimulus. The author believes these design criteria are critical to student survival and should be the primary focus of survival and combat instructors.

Chapter Six References

Applegate, R. (1994) *Bullseyes and Silhouettes Don't Shoot Back: Police Handgun Training Without the Use of Sights* Law & Order Magazine, October issue.

Breedlove, H. and Siddle, B. (1995) *How Stress Affects Vision and Shooting Stances*, Police Marksman Vol XX No. 3

Burroughs, W. (1993) *Dynamic Training Strategies*

Burroughs, W. (1993) Cited as a chapter resource.

Tanji, R. (1995) *Selection of Upper Torso Shooting Stances Utilizing Kinesiology Principles,* PPCT Research Publications

Vila, B. and Morrison, G. (1994) *Biological Limits of Police Combat Handgun Shooting Accuracy* American Journal of Police, Volume 13, No. 1

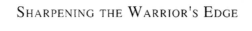

7

Survival Mindset

"Men are not afraid of death, they are afraid of dying."

Lord Moran, 1967

T hroughout the months of January, February and March of 1995, I watched in saddened fascination as my Grandmother prepared for her death. Cathryn Siddle was 87, exceptionally sharp of mind and memory, but had congestive heart failure. In the minds of her family, she was a matriarch who believed that values, principles and faith were not empty words, but the foundation of personal character.

In late March, her heart finally began to fail. She was admitted into the hospital with an apparent heart attack and was told that she would soon die. She ordered the physicians to take her off all medication and began to prepare the family for her death. Although her breathing was labored, she spoke lovingly and calmly about going home to heaven, seeing long gone friends and family, and she told me she wanted a fried brain sandwich as her "last meal."

I remember her calmness and focus on the tasks that needed to be completed for her death. No fear, no regrets, just absolute focus and concentration on finalizing all the details of her last minutes on earth.

Six hours later she began the process of dying. Her breathing increased in difficulty, but her mind remained sharp. At about 2:00 a.m. she started to fatigue of trying to breathe and began to pray out loud for Christ to take her home. At about 2:15 a.m. she suddenly got very indignant and <u>ordered</u> Christ to come and get her.

He did a short time later . . .

The majority of this text has examined quantitative research applied to learning principles and the effects of stress on performance and cognitive abilities. We now understand why specific skills are more conducive to stress than others. However, the research has yet to explain the intangible variables which true warriors seem to possess—the survival mindset.

A survival mindset denotes a presence of mind allowing the warrior to focus completely on the task of the moment. It is a mindset void of emotion, where perception, analysis, and response merge into one process. The warrior enters a state where perceptions are more acute, actions become reflexive, and concentration is not hampered by the potential of death. Most importantly, the warrior attains the ability to concentrate in presence of death and act reflexively without hesitation.

A true understanding of this state has been almost mysterious and elusive. However, we do know that a mental state is reached where anxiety and survival stress are kept under control during exceptional circumstances.

Identifying the psychological variables associated with a true survival mindset center around confidence in personal ability, personal values on life, belief in the mission, and faith systems. When in proper perspective, these values and beliefs create a mindset which controls survival stress, allowing the warrior to focus on the mission without distraction and respond without hesitation.

Unfortunately, values and beliefs are a product of life experiences. Instructors may find it difficult, if not impossible, to develop survival or combat instincts in a matter of weeks or months. However, we can state definitively that values and beliefs play a major role in adrenal and cardiac activity during combat. Students need to understand the scientific basis which values and beliefs have on their survival, so they can personally and privately, resolve these issues before they face combat.

Confidence: This text has focused extensively on the role of confidence from the instructor's perspective. However, we have not discussed the need for personal discipline to follow through with training. True warriors maintain a personal discipline to train without encouragement and without the need for extra compensation. They understand that disciplined training sharpens the warrior's edge. Training leads to an awareness of capabilities and confidence, which minimizes hesitation during combat. This factor is critical if "the difference between the living and the dieing is in the timing" (Lowery 1985).

Value of Life: The value of a human life is considered precious in today's society. Faith systems, legal systems, and personal morals are structured around protecting human life. However, sometimes warriors are required to take another life to protect themselves or another.

Some students will have difficulty in reconciling this possibility. Their value and belief systems may be so ingrained that the thought of killing another individual is as foreign as attempting suicide. However, when an individual chooses a profession where the potential to take another life is present, they voluntarily accept the responsibility to take a life to protect another or themselves. The fact is, "sometimes good people have to kill bad people to protect other good people" (Smith 1984).

Belief in the Mission: In today's society there are great risks in taking another life during war or in the line of duty. Law enforcement officers can expect to be litigated if they take another life, no matter how justified their actions were. Soldiers serve at the pleasure of politics, which change according to public opinion. But this is the arena which warriors voluntarily enter. This is the single element which makes today's warriors special. In an age where the words "honor" and "sacrifice" have little substantive meaning. Today's warriors willingly enter the arena to serve and protect. Dobson (1993) stated that the "human spirit is capable of withstanding enormous discomfort, including the prospect of death, if the circumstances make sense." However, the mission must make sense in the belief system of the students. If the students do not believe in the mission or the risks of the job outweigh the ultimate benefit to society, the students will hesitate in combat.

Faith Systems: "One who is a Samurai must before all things keep constantly in mind, by day and by night . . . the fact that he has to die." (Daidoji Yuzan 1600). The promise of death is a bridge which all living beings must cross. It is a fact of life, with only the cause and time a matter of speculation.

For warriors, death is challenged every time they go to work. When a police officer puts on his uniform, a soldier leaves on a mission, or a pilot enters the aircraft, the potential of death is lurking in the recesses of his conscious mind. Unfortunately, many warriors repress the thought of death and do not consider the full consequences of death until they are looking death in the eye. When this occurs, anxiety turns to fear, and fear creates hypervigilance.

The Japanese Samurai appeared to recognize this phenomenon more than any other culture of warriors. Their literature abounds with reflections on death. It appears that the Samurai were intuitively aware of the relationship between the fear of death and battlefield performance.

Today, some military special operations units have taken a serious look at the affects of faith on combat performance . In many units before soldiers go into combat, they are allowed time to speak to clergy to make peace with their Deity. The theory is that if soldiers are at peace with themselves, they will not be distracted in a deadly force encounter. The personal peace which comes with having a strong faith system keeps the soldiers' minds off the implications of death, reduces the additional stress (elevated heart rates), and allows them to focus their attention on the threat. This is why Deuteronomy 20:4, "For the Lord your God is the One who goes with you to fight for you, against your enemies to give you victory" is often prominantly displayed in the homes of warriors.

From a pure scientific perspective, this rationale makes sense. The promise of death is a bridge which all living things must cross. By bringing this potential into the open, officers and soldiers are forced to resolve the issue of death and faith before going into combat. Alexander, Groller and Morris (1990) state that when "training fails and reason is insufficient to save the day, the warrior reaches deep within, where his fundamental vision of self, God, or the universe, provides the winning edge. But those beliefs must already be there. Combat is not the place to be making major adjustments to your belief system."

There is a peace of mind resulting from a strong faith system. A peace of mind which lowers the heart rate, allowing for enhanced perceptual and mental processing, enhanced discretion and target selection, as well as the ability to complete more complex tasks.

A strong faith system minimizes the fear of dying, which Lord Moran believes created more anxiety than the thought of death. Galvin (1995) states, "This relief of anxiety allows the warrior to concentrate on the mission and staying alive." However, recent literature on the death process has suggested that God eases this by sending an angel or lost loved one to help cross the bridge. For some warriors, this thought, grounded by faith, provides a level of comfort which reduces the anxiety of "dying alone." However, we must remember that faith is "the substance of things hoped for, the evidence of things not seen" (Hebrews 11:1).

In the final hours of Cathryn Siddle's life, sleep was preciously rare due to her labored breathing. But after one short nap, she stated that Christ had come to her and told her that she would be going home soon. She told me she was looking forward to heaven, so she could "breathe normal." An aura of peace developed around her, with a clarity in thought and conversation which I would not have believed possible in the face of death.

A short time later while sitting alone with her, I noticed that she suddenly became very attentive to one corner of the hospital room. She was intent and scanning her eyes in a manner as if she was watching someone. I watched her for several minutes and then asked her if she was alright. She turned to me and stated that she couldn't be better. I am convinced that she saw someone in that corner who provided comfort and a peace of mind . . .

Chapter Seven Summary

This chapter attempted to establish a scientific basis for the need of values and belief systems in survival and combat training. The theoretical basis for this assertion is valid, but verifiable research to support this theory is yet to be documented. However, it is hard to argue that the presence of death does not have a profound effect on performance.

I have been researching the issues covered in this chapter for several years. After speaking to numerous police and correctional officers and special warfare and military combat pilots, I am convinced that belief and faith systems are the key to survival when training fails. But if death does come knocking, warriors can take comfort in knowing they will not be alone or the first to cross this bridge.

"Those of us who maintain a dangerous life-style will experience fear and anxiety. But, to do so, allows us to join a fraternity of those who have, since the beginning of man's time, endured . . . They endured. We endured. It is the cost of the privilege of such company."

Paul Whitesell 1988

Chapter Seven References

Alexander, J., Groller, R., and Morris, J. (1990)
The Warrior's Edge, Morrow Publishing.

Dobson, J. (1993) *When God Doesn't Make Sense*,
Tyndale House Publishers.

Deuteronomy 20:4 *Holy Bible*

Galvin, R. (1995) *Training Quote.*

Hebrews 11:1 *Holy Bible.*

Lord Moran, (1967) *The Anatomy of Courage*,
Houghton Miffin Company.

Lowry, D. (1985) *Autumn Lightning,* Shambala

Whitesell, P. (1988) *The Psychology of Intimidation and
Physical Conflict in the Police Profession*,
PPCT Research Publications.

Yuzan, Daidoji, (circa 1600) *The Code of the Samurai*,
Reprinted and edited by Sadler, A. (1941)
Charles E. Tuttle Company.

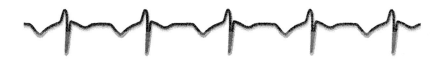

References

Introduction References

Alexander, J., Groller, R., and Morris, J. (1990)
The Warrior's Edge, Morrow Publishing
National Research Council, (1988) *Enhancing Human Performance*: National Academy Press
National Research Council, (1991) *In the Mind's Eye*: National Academy Press

Chapter One References

Guthrie, E.R.(1952) *The Psychology of Learning*: Harper & Row.
Pargman, Dan. (1986). *Stress and Motor Performance: Understanding and Coping.*
Millman, Dan. (1979). *The Warrior Athlete.*
Rose, Colin. (1987) *Accelerated Learning*: Dell Publishing.
Schmidt, Richard A. (1991). *Motor Learning and Performance*, Human Kinetics.
Siddle, Bruce. (1991). *Survival Learning Theory Instructional Outline*,PPCT Management Systems, Inc.

Chapter Two References

Deporter, B. and Hernacki, M. (1992). *Quantum Learning*: Dell Publishing.

Hontz, Tom (1995). *Vertical Versus Horizontal Decision Making For Officer Survival Training*

Johnson, George (1991) *In The Palaces of Memory*: Vintage Books.

McConnell, J.V. (1966) As cited in *Accelerated Learning*, Dell Publishing

Millman, Dan (1979). *The Warrior Spirit, Mind Body and Spirit*: Stillpoint Publishing.

Moravec, Hans, (1992). *Minds With Mobility*, Discovery Magazine, (1992, November Issue).

Rose, Colin (1987). *Accelerated Learning*, Dell Publishing.

Schneider, A and Tarshis, B. (1986) *Physiological Psychology,* Random House

Unger, George (1970) As cited in *Accelerated Learning,* Dell Publishing

Chapter Three References

Bryan, W.L. and Harter, N. (1899) *Studies in the Psysiology and Psychology of Telegraphic Language.* Psychological Review, 4, 27-53.

Cassidy, W. L., (1978). *Quick or Dead;* Boulder Paladin Press.

Cratty, B. J. (1973). *Movement Behavior and Motor Learning.*

Garcia, R. (1989). *A Field Study of Side Handle Baton Techniques;* PPCT Research Publications.

Guthrie, E. R. (1952) *The Psychology of Learning*, Harper & Row.

Knapp, B. N. (1961). *A Note on Skill*, Occupation Psychology 35.

Levitt, S. and Gutin, B. (1971) *Multiple Choice Reaction Time and Movement Time During Physical Exertion,* Research Quarterly 42.

Levitt, S. (1972) *The Effects of Exercise Induced Activation Upon Simple, Two-Choice and Five-Choice Reaction Time and Movement Time.* Doctoral Dissertation.

Poulton, E. C. (1957). *On Prediction in Skilled Movements,* Psychological Bulletin 54.

Sage, G. H. (1984). *Motor Learning and Control; A Neural Psychological Approach,* William C. Brown Publishers.

Schmidt, R. A. (1991) *Motor Learning & Performance; From Principles to Practice,* Human Kinetics.

Shelton, T.O. and Mahoney, M.J. (1978) *The Content and Effect of Psyching-Up Strategies in Weight Lifters,* Cognitive Therapy & Research -2 (1979)

Weinberg, R.S.; Gould, D. & Jackson, A., *Expectations and Performance: An Empirical Test of Bandura's Self-Efficacy Theory.* Journal of Sport Psychology.

Westmoreland, H. (1989). *An Examination of Stress Shooting Stances;* PPCT Research Publications.

Chapter Four References

Applegate, R. (1943) *Kill or Get Killed,* Paladin Press

Cassidy, W. L., (1978). *Quick or Dead;* Boulder Paladin Press

Cratty, B. J. (1973). *Movement Behavior and Motor Learning,* Lea and Febiger

Easterbrook, J.A. (1959) *The Effects of Emotion on Cue-Utilization and the Organization of Behavior.* Psychological Review.

Garcia, R. (1989). *A Field Study of Side Handle Baton Techniques;* PPCT Research Publications

Guthrie, E. R. (1952) *The Psychology of Learning*, Harper & Row

Gutin, B. and Levitt, S. (1971). *Multiple Choice Reaction Time and Movement Time during Physical Exertion;* Research Quarterly

Knapp, B. N. (1961). *A Note on Skill,* Occupation Psychology 35

Levitt, S. (1972). *The Effects of Exercise Induced Activation Upon Simple, Two-Choice, and Five-Choice Reaction Time and Movement Time;* Doctoral Dissertation, Columbia University

McGivern, E. (1932 original) (1975, 1984) *Fast and Fancy Revolver Shooting;* New Win Publishing, Inc.

Pargman, (1986) *Stress and Motor Performance: Understanding and Coping*, Mouvment Publications.

Parsons, S. (1993) *Improving Short Term Memory Retention of Visual Short Term Sensory Store Stimulus;* PPCT Research Publications

Poulton, E. C. (1957). *On Prediction in Skilled Movements*, Psychological Bulletin 54

Sage, G. H. (1984). *Motor Learning and Control; A Neural Psychological Approach*, William C. Brown Publishers

Schmidt, R. A. (1991) *Motor Learning & Performance; From Principles to Practice*, Human Kinetics

Weltman, G. and Egstrom, G. H. (1966). *Human Factors*

Chapter Five References

Alexander, J., Groller, R. and Morris, J. (1990) *The Warrior's Edge*, Morrow Publishing.

Benson, H. (1975) *The Relaxation Response*, Avon Books

Denis, M. (1985) *Visual Imagery and the Use of Mental Practice in the Development of Motor Skills.* Unpublished Doctoral Dissertation.

Janis, I.L. and Mann, L. (1977) *Decision Making: A Psychological Analysis of Conflict, Choice and Commitment.*

Janis, I.L., Defares, P. and Grossman, P. (1983) *Selye's Guide to Stress Research,* Van Nostrauz Reinholz Publishing.

McGrath, J.E. (1970) *Social and Psychological Factors in Stress,* Holt, Rinehart and Winston

Murphy, S. and Jowdy, D. (1992) *Advances in Sports Psychology,* (Chapter 11), Human Kinetics Publishing.

Pargman, (1986) *Stress and Motor Performance: Understanding and Coping.* Mouvment Publications.

Porter, K. and Foster, J. (1986) *The Mental Athlete,* William C. Brown Publishers.

Schmidt, R. (1987) *Motor Control and Learning,* 2nd Edition, Human Kinetics.

Whitesell, P., (1989) *The Psychology of Intimidation and the Physical Conflict in the Police Profession,* PPCT Research Publications.

Chapter Six References

Applegate, R. (1994) *Bullseyes and Silhouettes Don't Shoot Back: Police Handgun Training Without the Use of Sights* Law & Order Magazine, October issue.

Breedlove, H. and Siddle, B. (1995) *How Stress Affects Vision and Shooting Stances,* Police Marksman Vol XX No. 3

Burroughs, W. (1993) *Dynamic Training Strategies.*

Burroughs, W. (1993) Cited as a chapter resource.

Tanji, R. (1995) *Selection of Upper Torso Shooting Stances Utilizing Kinesiology Principles,* PPCT Research Publications

Vila, B. and Morrison, G. (1994) *Biological Limits of Police Combat Handgun Shooting Accuracy* American Journal of Police, Volume 13, No. 1

Chapter Seven References

Alexander, J., Groller, R., and Morris, J. (1990) *The Warrior's Edge,* Morrow Publishing.

Dobson, J. (1993) *When God Doesn't Make Sense,* Tyndale House Publishers.

Deuteronomy 20:4 *Holy Bible.*

Galvin, R. (1995) *Training Quote.*

Hebrews 11:1 *Holy Bible.*

Lord Moran, (1967) *The Anatomy of Courage,* Houghton Miffin Company.

Lowry, D. (1985) *Autumn Lightning,* Shambala

Whitesell, P. (1988) *The Psychology of Intimidation and Physical Conflict in the Police Profession,* PPCT Research Publications.

Yuzan, Daidoji, (circa 1600) *The Code of the Samurai,* Reprinted and edited by Sadler, A. (1941). Charles E. Tuttle Company